india's vegetarian cooking

monisha bharadwaj

kyle books

photography of India by Jenner Zimmermann

food photography by Will Heap

india's
vegetarian
cooking

monisha bharadwaj

This edition published in 2006 by Kyle Books
An imprint of Kyle Cathie Limited
www.kylecathie.com

ISBN 1 904920 41 1
ISBN (13-digit) 978 1 904920 41 0

Designer Geoff Hayes
Proofreader Sarah Epton
Indexer Alex Corrin
Americanizer Delora Jones
Production Sha Huxtable & Alice Holloway

Bharadwaj, Monisha.
India's Vegetarian Cooking: A regional guide/Monisha Bharadwaj
1.Cookery, Vegetarian

Library of Congress Control Number: 2006935934

1 2 3 4 5

Color reproduction by Colourscan
Printed in China by C+C Offset Printing Co. Ltd.

contents

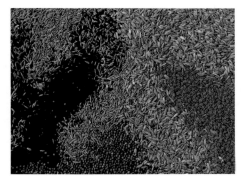

introduction

My introduction to regional cooking began at an early age. As children, my parents took my brother and me traveling around India at every given opportunity. Aged six, I had eaten the finest Gujarati thali in Rajkot, by eight I had tasted the choicest tandoori foods in Amritsar, and by 12, we had covered most of south India with its steaming hot Kanjeevaram idlis and chutneys. Of course the extensive range that I was exposed to was not something to wonder about at the time. I sort of took it for granted and slowly my love of food and cooking developed. It was almost like a bud opening into a flower, the myriad taste sensations gradually becoming more and more distinct as I grew up.

Later I went to the Bombay Catering College, the finest in the country at the time, and was taught about the theory as well as the practical side of cooking—classic recipes, quantity cooking, nutrition, and how to standardize recipes. Here again regional cooking was important. The nuances of Keralan cuisine were set apart from those of Kashmiri cooking and the history, traditions, and rituals associated with food, which are all so essential in India, began to come alive.

Growing up in Mumbai, arguably India's most cosmopolitan city, meant that I had friends from every state in the country. Their families had moved to Mumbai (or Bombay as it was then called) for work or education and I remember us spending a lot of time at each other's homes. Often this was to share a family meal which meant that, almost every weekend, I was eating delicious south Indian, Parsee, Gujarati, or Punjabi food. They in turn loved the Maharashtrian and Goan delicacies at my home. I never failed to ask their moms and grandmothers for special recipes and, by the time I was 16, I had a formidable recipe collection of my own. Later I would enchant my family with delicious lentils and curries from around the country. When I joined the Catering College, I began practicing classic French cooking at home because it formed a large portion of our syllabus. My friends and relatives were often willing volunteers for tastings and adventurous cooking.

Little has changed. I still ask for recipes when I have had a fantastic meal and most cooks are flattered. And I still have many volunteers willing to come over for dinner when I do recipe trials.

Much of my own home cooking is vegetarian because that was how I was brought up. All my favorite foods are from the vegetarian world. I also feel happier, healthier, and more energetic after a vegetarian meal.

Indian cooking is an art form—subtle, delicate, and beautiful. The variety is endless and, in a country that is home to billions of people, there is a new way of cooking every few miles you travel. I have often said that it is almost like living in many countries at the same time, so great is the variety of food, language, dress, and custom. Even within particular regions, each household will often have their own recipe for the same dish, one that has been passed down the generations in that home. Over time, it will have been adapted so that hundreds of recipes exist for the same dish.

deeper knowledge about food

Having said that, original recipes do exist and every variation is still true to this original. Cooks are taught, as I was, to use their senses while cooking. I can only cook if I smell, touch, and see my ingredients and appreciate all the qualities of the food I am working with. Often an Indian cook will know what amount of seasoning to add simply by the aroma of the dish. It is important to know exactly when a fruit is ripe, what it will taste like when cooked, and also, very importantly, how it will nourish and heal the body.

A large part of Indian cooking is that food should be perfectly balanced. As children we are told that certain foods cool us in the summer or that particular food combinations make us feel lethargic or dull. Ayurveda, the Indian system of holistic healing, is a natural inclusion in the everyday process of eating and cooking. Knowing when to cut open a melon or how to dry its seeds to make a nutritious snack for the children are skills that are passed down as fact. There is also a vast body of knowledge that tells us how foods affect our moods and feelings and we are taught to eat for positive well-being.

short history of vegetarianism in india

Almost 85 percent of India is Hindu and, because of religion, vegetarian. Not all Hindus are vegetarian, as caste and community also affect this choice. Some of my strict Brahmin ancestors ate fish simply because they lived near the coast around Goa. Most non-vegetarians will eat meat or fish a few times a week or even just once, firstly because it is expensive and secondly because the choice of vegetables, lentils, beans, and dairy products is so vast that there is an endless variety for each day of the year. Vegetarian food is also considered healthier than meat because it is easier to digest. Few people today believe that a vegetarian diet is lacking in protein; in fact, the lentils and beans that are an essential part of the Indian diet provide an extremely good source of protein.

India is already well-known for its tradition of vegetarianism which has a history going back almost two millennia. During the Vedic period, almost 5,000 years ago, animals were hunted for food, and meat was eaten regularly by the warrior community of Kshatriyas. The anti-meat eating sentiment began to be felt at the end of the Vedic period. This coincided with the rise of Buddhism and Jainism whose founders, the Buddha and Lord Mahavira respectively, taught their followers the doctrines of nonviolence. As more and more people began to convert to these newer beliefs, Hindu priests, fearing that a great number of their people would convert, also began preaching against the killing of animals. They adopted "ahimsa" or non-violence and followed a vegetarian diet, regarding it as superior to the older Brahminical ideas of animal sacrifice.

essentials of indian vegetarian cooking

What binds the cuisines of the different regions of India is the use of spices. Used originally to preserve foods, they are now added in extremely complex combinations to bring out the best flavors and textures in a dish. Grains and rice provide the carbohydrate element. Many types of rice have been known in India for the past 5,000 years and references to them can be found in the ancient texts. Protein is eaten in the form of lentils and beans, and every Indian kitchen will have a myriad of jars full of colorful lentils and legumes.

influences

Over the centuries, several dynasties came to India and built new empires. With these foreign powers came an amazing variety of cooking styles and ingredients. New world ingredients such as tomatoes, chiles, and potatoes became everyday food in many parts of India. English cooking influenced areas such as Calcutta and Madras, which were strongholds of the Raj. French cooking became a part of the daily diet in Pondicherry, and Goan food showed influences of the Portuguese style. The Parsees who came from Iran brought their own unique food combinations and became a part of the local population as did the Jews. North Indian cooking was vastly influenced by the Afghani rulers who founded the Mughal Empire. It is this ability to absorb all influences, turn them around, and take ownership of the new styles that makes Indian cooking so fascinating and vibrant and a constantly evolving melee.

Spices which today signal the advent of cooking are found in abundance in India. Most of the world's spices are grown here and many have been studied not just for their culinary uses but also for their healing powers. Spices and fresh herbs are very intricately woven into Indian life, featuring in food, prayer, and medical treatments. For example, turmeric is revered as an antiseptic, asafetida helps with flatulence, carom counters nausea, and ginger is an aphrodisiac. Fenugreek and cumin seeds are given to nursing mothers to aid secretion. How a spice is used and when it is added to the pot can easily reveal what province of India the food is from and for whom it has been cooked.

equipment

A rural Indian kitchen and an urban one are quite different in the way that they function, but some functional tools and utensils are essential to every Indian kitchen, throughout the world. A spicebox is a must; this handy box has small compartments and tiny individual spoons for the main spices used in everyday cooking, including turmeric, chili powder, cumin, coriander, black mustard seeds, and asafetida.

Most Indian cooks prefer to use a selection of stainless steel, aluminum, brass, and iron utensils and, due to the intense heat, the bottoms of these pots and pans are reinforced with a thick layer of the same metal or one of copper. A kadhai, or heavy Indian wok, is found in every kitchen. Ideal in shape and thickness, it can be used for stir-frying or deep-frying and ensures even, nonstick cooking. Kadhais are available in many sizes and qualities. Look for a thick, heavy aluminum one with a handle that makes it easier to work with. Highly decorative, kitchen-to-table kadhais look pretty but they are not very heavy and can heat up too quickly. Other popular utensils are rimmed, straight-sided, upright vessels called degchis. No Indian kitchen can function without a grinder of some sort. The vast panorama of spice pastes and powders, chutneys, and masalas demand a heavy-duty method of reducing whole spices, fruits, herbs, and nuts to a smooth blend. Stone slabs with a heavy, rounded grinding stone are still used and are actually preferred by many cooks as the pastes made on them need less water and are often more concentrated. However, these are being rapidly replaced by powerful electric blenders, which

have various attachments for dry and wet grinding and can reduce the hardest spices to a fine, soft powder. They make an invaluable investment. You can also use a coffee grinder to grind small quantities of spices very effectively. However, remember to wash it well afterwards or you might end up with coriander-flavored coffee the next time you use your machine! Very small amounts of spice seeds, made brittle by dry-roasting, can be ground in a mortar with a pestle and I use mine to make fresh garam masala and other

spice blends; I need the spice powders to be fine for some dishes and coarse for others. Food processors that can grate, chop, and knead are also becoming more and more popular in Indian kitchens, though many cooks genuinely believe that traditional methods produce tastier food.

In India, where coconut inspires the cuisine of many states, there will be a coconut-scraper in the majority of southern and eastern homes. This is a flat, wooden base to which a sickle-shaped blade is attached. It has a serrated fan at the end, which is used to scrape out the white flesh from the coconut shell. The blade is also used to chop meat and vegetables. This whole device is placed on the floor and one has to sit on the wooden base to use it. Coconut can also be grated effectively in a food processor after breaking open the shell and prying away the flesh. Small stainless steel or brass graters are used for grating ginger and garlic and you can always use a garlic press.

One of the most versatile tools available to an Indian cook is a pressure cooker. Although they seem to have gone out of fashion in the West, they are used to make everything from curries to puddings. As they reduce cooking times drastically and give a perfectly finished product, they are invaluable to anyone who wants to rustle up a meal in minutes.

Another must is a refrigerator. As Indian food retains its flavor even after freezing, it can be prepared well in advance and stored for later use. In very hot weather, along with the usual meat, milk, and vegetables, flour goes into the fridge, too.

what is a curry?

Many people in my demonstrations ask me whether "curry" is an Anglicized dish that does not exist in India. I have to say that hardly any Indian meal is complete without a curry. The word comes from the Tamil "kari" which means gravy or vegetable dish. In south Indian curries it is based on a blend of coconut and tamarind, while in the north it is made from a range of mild spices. There is really no such thing as a Madras curry or even Madras curry powder as the terms seem too general for the hundreds of variations that exist.

Many things are important when judging a curry. Firstly think of the consistency: is it too thick or too watery? A good curry should be fairly thick and, as I have often said in this book, like custard. A thin curry will not support an even blend of spices whereas too thick a one will not moisten the accompanying rice or bread sufficiently.

Secondly think of color. Turmeric, chiles, tamarind, and coriander are some of the ingredients that add color to a curry. They add flavor and aroma as well. Generally curries can be white (as in a Kashmiri yogurt-based yakhni), red (as in a makhani), yellow (as in many kormas), and green (as in a south Indian nilgiri). The oil used also varies from region to region giving each curry a unique fragrance. Many parts of the south use peanut oil or coconut oil. In Bengal, it is mustard oil. Over most of the country it is ghee although younger cooks are now choosing healthier options such as sunflower oil.

All good curries begin with patience. In the north, a basic curry starts with the heating of the oil. Then the seed spices are added to release their aromatic oils. The onions, ginger, garlic, and tomatoes go in next to add moisture. The pan is now ready to receive the powdered spices so that they do not burn. The main ingredient, plus salt and a little water are added next to obtain the right consistency. Controlled heat and an eye for the right texture and color are equally important.

Thus curries are made in steps, almost like building blocks. The blocks can be moved around and rearranged in countless ways to give never ending recipes that tease the tastebuds and create a burst of complementary flavors.

and finally

I have enjoyed writing this book immensely because it is really the way I cook and eat on a daily basis. I truly believe that vegetarian food can be immensely exciting, infinitely diverse, and wonderfully fresh and healthy. I hope that my readers discover the many pleasures of Indian regional vegetarian cooking through this book, as I have done through the years.

basic recipe

Ginger-garlic paste

Ginger and garlic are almost always used together in Indian cooking. To make the ginger-garlic paste used in this book, take equal quantities of each and whiz in a blender until smooth. I usually make this paste in big batches and freeze it in thin sheets between plastic. Of course you will have to put the frozen sheets of ginger and garlic in big freezer containers or else everything from your ice cream to ice cubes will smell weird! Just break off bits when you need them and add straight into the pan.

ayurveda

According to Ayurveda, foods have healing properties that are categorized by "rasa" or taste. The word rasa means both taste and emotion and this aspect of food has a deep effect on our physical and mental health. The six tastes, namely sweet, sour, bitter, astringent, salty, and pungent, all have specific effects on each individual constitution and can contribute differently to each person's well-being. Taste is said to have both long term and short term effects. Tastes can be light or heavy, moist or dry. Light tastes include rice, ghee, and mung dal, which are easier to digest than heavy tastes, such as black lentils or bananas.

The unique combination of energy present in each individual at birth is that person's constitution or "prakruti." Your prakruti is determined by the proportion and balance of the five elements, namely earth, fire, water, air, and ether, in your body and therefore no two people are alike. Ayurveda believes that there is no single path to health and each person must be treated individually depending upon the prakruti. There are no general rules about which foods to eat because each of us must learn to be aware of the effects that different foods have upon our mind, body, and spirit. Indians also believe that peaceful surroundings and a quiet mind at mealtimes help to boost immunity, aid digestion, and conserve stamina for future tasks.

The five elements—air, fire, water, earth, and ether—exist in nature, in food, and even within our bodies. Air promotes health, fire is purification, water signifies movement and fluidity, earth symbolizes energy and fecundity, and ether or space echoes with vibrations of the Divine. When all the elements are maintained in balance in our bodies, good health follows.

The three basic constitutions are determined by a combination of energies called "doshas." The constitutions are Vata (governed by air and ether), Pitta (governed by fire and water), and Kapha (governed by water and earth). Very loosely, if you are a Vata constitution you will find that you suffer from wind, have dry hair and skin, and that your hands and feet are often cold. A Pitta constitution means that you will generate a lot of internal heat, you may be moody and angry, and you are frequently thirsty. Kapha produces a lot of mucus, is often afflicted by coughs and colds, and finds it easy to gain weight. If we understand our own constitution and choose foods as well as a lifestyle accordingly, we provide ourselves with the best chance of good health. Sometimes two doshas form a combination in a single individual and at times, all the doshas are present making it a balanced or "tridoshic" constitution.

All Indians grow up with this kind of knowledge and understand when to eat what foods for optimum health. We are also taught to respect nature, and everywhere in India, great importance is placed on seasonal foods. You would never expect to find mangoes in the winter because they are a summer fruit and this is when they are at their best. An out of season fruit or vegetable will not have adequate healing and nourishing properties. At the center of Ayurvedic nutrition is the awareness of "agni" or the digestive fire. In the winter, this demands heavier foods such as grains and proteins, or warm foods such as honey and herb teas. In the summer, agni is at a low and we feel like eating fresher, lighter foods such as salads and yogurt.

Eight rules of an ayurvedic diet

Prakruti—Choose a combination of foods based upon their nature, that is their inherent heaviness or lightness. (Meat is heavy to digest, vegetables are light.)

Karana—The processing of foods affects their influence on our bodies. Generally, cooked foods are easier to digest, with the exception of fruits and some vegetables. Frying adds heaviness whereas stir-frying helps introduce some lightness. Microwave cooking destroys "prana" or the life force of foods.

Samyoga—Combine foods healthily and never mix contrary foods. Fish and dairy are not combined as they both need a different rate of acid secretion as well as concentration of acid in the stomach for proper digestion.

Rashi—Control the quantity of food you eat according to your constitution.

Desha—Eat according to your environment. Consider the seasons and factors such as humidity and pollution.

Kala—Be attentive to the time of eating. Eat only when the previous meal has had a chance to be properly digested.

Upayoga Sanstha—Follow the golden rules of eating. Eat food when it is hot. Concentrate on eating rather than on laughing, talking, reading, or on distractions. Be calm and unhurried, and smoking or drinking too much during a meal is not advisable.

Upabhokta—Every person must decide for herself or himself about what to eat, depending upon how one feels. Never force yourself or eat against your instinct.

a religious perspective on food

"The purchaser of flesh performs himsa (violence) by his wealth; he who eats flesh does so by enjoying its taste; the killer does himsa by actually tying and killing the animal. Thus, there are three forms of killing: he who brings flesh or sends for it, he who cuts off the limbs of an animal, and he who purchases, sells, or cooks flesh and eats it—all of these are to be considered meat-eaters."
Mahabharata

Most Hindus are vegetarian due to various reasons. Firstly, they consider that Ahimsa, or the law of non-violence, is a Hindu's first duty towards God and all of God's creation must be respected. The love and protection of animals is central to Hinduism and even the ancients associated each deity with an animal with a view to its protection and conservation. Hindu gods and goddesses each have an animal with them as a personal vehicle or companion. Therefore Shiva has the bull, Durga the lion or tiger, Ganesh the mouse, and Kartikeya the peacock. Many Hindus feel that killing and eating animals will be disrespectful to the gods who so overtly protect and cherish all beings.

Secondly, they believe that all one's actions, including one's choice of food, have Karmic consequences. The Karma theory is about reaping what you sow, so that each of our actions is rewarded or punished at a later date, sometimes even in following lifetimes. By being a part of the cycle of inflicting pain and death, even indirectly, on other living creatures one brings upon oneself the suffering one has caused to others, in equal measure. Similarly, a good deed will be repaid in equal measure almost like a blessing when one needs it most.

Hindus also believe that food is a source of health and healing, and can govern our moods and emotions. By eating the flesh of animals, we eat their innermost being, and introduce into our bodies all their anxieties, fears and instincts. This can bring us into a lower realm of consciousness where spiritual awareness, which is the chief purpose of the Hindu way of life, becomes impossible.

Studies have proved that a vegetarian diet can provide a greater range of nutrients and fewer toxins. Vegetarians are usually less prone to major illnesses and lead longer, healthier lives. Many vegetarians are also nonsmokers, have more balanced weights than non vegetarians, and consume less alcohol. Also, a vegetarian diet is more ecologically friendly. As Albert Einstein said, "Nothing will benefit human health and increase chances for survival of life on Earth as much as the evolution to a vegetarian diet." Animals becoming extinct, air and water pollution all have links to the slaughter of animals. More land is required for the breeding of animals for consumption than for the growing of an equal quantity of protein-rich plant foods. If we are to save our planet, it is important for us all to adopt a vegetarian diet.

Having said this, there is a great variety of beliefs within India. The Christians, Jews, and Parsees will eat meat while most Hindus will not. Within the Hindus, some communities such as the Jains are very particular and will not eat even onions or garlic. This is due to the belief that these heat-producing foods can excite the passions and lead the mind away from a constant awareness of spirituality. Most

Hindu temples will only serve vegetarian food and in many traditional communities, religious celebrations such as weddings will have vegetarian feasts. In some Hindu homes, kitchen utensils for the preparation of meat are kept separately and never mixed with the "vegetarian" utensils.

It is perhaps true that for some Indians, being vegetarian is itself their dharma or religious practice. However, there are many Hindu communities where meat or fish is very common, especially in the coastal states of Kerala and West Bengal. In Bengal, even religious feasts in honor of the Mother Goddess Kali include several meat and fish dishes. Muslims all over the country eat meat and in north India, the Punjabis are renowned for their chicken fare such as tandoori chicken. Nevertheless, most people around the world see India as being a perfect haven for vegetarians, a land full of rice, wheat, beans and lentils, vegetables and fruit. In many meat-eating Indian families, meat is usually a Sunday afternoon feast and is eaten only on that one day of the week. For some other families, meat—and this most often means chicken or mutton (lamb from older sheep)—is eaten a few times a year at weddings or celebrations.

Another practice found in many middle class families in northern, western, and central India is that the women of the house will not eat meat whereas the men will. Eating meat is sometimes associated with masculinity, or with the baser instincts to which it is thought that men are more prone, probably going with the belief that to eat an animal is to turn into an animal oneself.

a synergy with the land

The ancient people who lived in India were nature worshippers. The sun brought warmth and light, the rain fed crops, the earth seemed to mysteriously provide food and the air carried health and comfort. As time went on, the five elements (fire, water, earth, air, and ether) became sacred and held a central position in religion and worship. Even today, the five elements are given a special place and they are at the core of many Indian arts, philosophies, and sciences.

Thousands of years ago the process of procreation generated awe and respect. People realized that it is the female who conceives and bears both males and females. The similarity between the mother giving birth to a child as a result of intercourse and the earth sprouting plants after the sowing of seeds glorified both the mother and the earth to a divine status. Worship of fertility was linked with the worship of the mother-goddess. The earth was looked upon as a mother and was symbolically worshipped as such. The terms mother-earth and motherland (Matrubhoomi) are still used today. The ancients had a high regard for the earth and worshipped it as Bhoomi Devi or Earth Goddess, always female because of her fertility and ability to produce plants, trees, and crops from deep within herself. Bhoomi Devi had to be kept happy so that she would keep offering her riches. Several stories, rituals, and celebrations developed around her and her generosity.

According to later legend, while Siddhartha who later became the Buddha, sat meditating under the bodhi tree, Mara the Tempter released his mighty armies. But Siddhartha fearlessly continued to meditate. When asked for his account of merit, he touched the fingers of his right hand to the earth and said, "The very Earth is my witness." The Earth Goddess materialized at once and agreed that she had witnessed every act of merit that this monk had committed, over several incarnations. Then she wrung out her long hair where the merit had been stored in the form of sparkling water. The water created such a flood that Mara's armies were all drowned in it. In Eastern philosophies, the earth is often held as witness, a silent sentinel who observes everything.

In the great epic, *The Ramayana*, Rama's wife, Sita, was said to be born out of the earth, making her an elemental woman and in the story, when she is asked to prove her chastity, she cannot bear this humiliation and asks to return to her mother. The earth opens up at her feet and accepts her back.

To this day, an Indian dancer will begin a practice session by doing a "namaskaar" or paying obeisance to the earth. This act is deeply symbolic as the dancer asks for blessings from the primeval Mother as well as for forgiveness for touching her with one's feet, an act considered disrespectful by all Indians.

Harvest festivals all over the world celebrate the fecundity of the earth. In southern India "Pongal" is celebrated as a happy four-day harvest festival with the cooking of newly harvested rice. Cows and bullocks, who are associated with the land through grass, milk, or tilling, are beautifully decorated with flowers and fed on "pongal" which is also a candy made of rice and jaggery (palm sugar).

The four days of the festival each have their own significance, and separate deities are worshipped each day. On the first day the Rain God is worshipped. The day begins with an oil bath and in the evening there is a ceremonial bonfire. The second day is that of the Sun God. The place where the ritual worship is carried out is cleaned and decorated with floor paintings called kolams. Sweet "pongal" is cooked and offered, on a new banana leaf, to the Sun God in gratitude for showering his blessings on the land and for the bountiful harvest. The third day is that of the cattle worship. On this day, the cattle are decorated and paraded in the village amidst much fanfare and celebration. The final day is when birds are worshipped.

In northern India, the picture is quite different. In Punjab, the granary of India, wheat is the main winter crop, which is sown in October and harvested in March or April. In January, as the fields fill up with the new harvest, farmers celebrate the festival of Lohri. This falls in January at a time when the earth is farthest away from the sun. The festival coincides with the point when the earth begins its journey towards the sun and therefore heralds the move towards seasonal warmth and sunshine.

At dusk, huge bonfires are lit in the harvested fields and people gather around the rising flames, circle the bonfire, and throw puffed rice or new corn into the fire, sing popular folk songs, and dance in joy. This is a ritual to honor Agni, the Fire God, to bless the land

with abundance and prosperity. Lohri celebrates fertility and the joy of life.

An ancient belief that is still practiced in India today is Vastu Shastra, the science of land, earth, and buildings. It takes into account how the five elements will affect the construction of a building and the luck it will bring to its owners. Vastu Shastra depends largely upon astrology and the eight directions. Each direction is ruled by a deity. The North is ruled by Kubera, the god of Wealth, and according to the science of Vastu Shastra, this is the direction for the storage of wealth in a home. Money, jewelry, and all cupboards that hold valuable possessions should be placed in the northern part of the house near the southern or western wall and facing the east or the north to attract even more wealth.

There are many factors around the building that affect the flow of money and wealth into it. One such factor is the existence of a large open space directly in front of the house. Large empty spaces are governed by the largely malefic planet Rahu (in Hindu astrology), which suppresses growth and prosperity. Another factor is the presence of a road end across the home, that is, if the home is at a T-junction, Rahu will see to it that all the family wealth comes to a dead end and that the inhabitants of the house will face great financial difficulty. If there are such problematic areas in front of the house, they can be corrected by planting beautiful, flowering shrubs or better still, the holy basil (Tulsi) plant that is considered so auspicious all over India and grows well in the summer all over the world.

My main focus in the north has been on the states of Punjab, Uttar Pradesh, Kashmir, and Delhi. The overall style of cooking in the north is fairly similar among the states but, perhaps because this area of India has seen the most turbulent phases of history and the most number of invasions, the cuisine is a wonderful blend of many cultures.

punjab

A large number of Indians who live outside of India are Punjabi in origin. In many families, ancestors several generations ago left India in search of better prospects and a new way of life. They carried with them the culture of India so much so that today, in many parts of the world when talking of Indian cooking, it is Punjabi food that is being dissussed. Rich onion- and tomato-flavored curries or the delicious tandoori foods that are cooked slowly in a clay oven called the tandoor, even the nans and parathas, all originate in Punjab. The Punjabis, both the Hindus and the Sikhs, are possibly the most fun-loving community of India. Ever ready to celebrate with food, drink, and dancing, their cuisine is rich and liberally flavored.

It has sometimes been said that, because much of Punjab is agricultural and rural farming communities abound, the cooking of this state is rather unsophisticated. I would say that, in order to satisfy these hard-working people, the cuisine is hearty and wholesome. In fact, most Indians love Punjabi cooking, and restaurants in this style do great business in every Indian town and city. Most non-Punjabis think of this cuisine as being for an occasional treat and look forward to a meal laced with ghee and cream and accompanied by fried treats such as samosas and pakoras. Ingredients that you would commonly find in a Punjabi kitchen are beans such as chickpeas and red kidney beans; and black lentils; vegetables such as cauliflower, potatoes, peas, and turnips; and whole wheat flour to make many kinds of breads. The Punjab grows a lot of wheat and was known as the granary of India for a long time.

kashmir

This is one of the most beautiful states of India, resplendent with green valleys, flowing waterfalls, pine forests, and fruit-filled orchards. Due to its proximity to the Himalayas it was the natural passage to India for many invaders. Its cuisine is therefore a mix of Indian, Persian, and Afghani styles. There are two distinct communities who live in Kashmir: the Muslims and the Hindu Brahmins who are known as "Kashmiri Pundits." The cuisine of Kashmir makes the most of the local produce such as walnuts, dried apricots, and pistachios. As it is a hilly state, not too many vegetables and herbs are grown, and the cuisine is largely meat-based. Spices such as dried ginger powder, fennel powder, and saffron, which grow in Kashmir, are used. Yogurt forms the base for many curries. The true cooking of Kashmir can be seen in the Wazawan style which is fragrant with spices including cardamom, cloves, and cinnamon. Even today, the master chefs of Kashmir are the descendants of the traditional chefs from Samarkand, the Wazas. The original Wazas came to India with the ruler Timur when he entered India in the 15th century. The royal Wazawan, comprised of 36 courses, is a feast that few can get through.

The meal begins with the ritual of washing the hands, then the "tramis" or dishes filled with food begin to arrive. The entrées are eaten with a sticky, dense variety of rice which is prized. Much of the Wazawan is meat-based as this is a sign of affluence but vegetarian dishes with lotus root or potatoes are also served. The meal is washed down with Kahwa tea which is flavored with saffron, cinnamon, and almonds.

uttar pradesh

Two of India's most sacred Hindu cities lie in this state. Varanasi and Allahabad are thronged with pilgrims each year and it is not surprising that Uttar Pradesh has a rich and varied vegetarian cuisine. All religious food in India must only include those ingredients

which are considered acceptable. An awareness of what is and what is not acceptable is inculcated in each generation by word of mouth. However, Uttar Pradesh does have a nonvegetarian repertoire of food as well. The vegetarian food is light and nutritious and largely free of the heavy spices that dominate much of north Indian cooking. Coriander and cumin are favored while legumes and dried legumes form the base of many curries. One of the most famous styles of cooking that originates from this state is the Awadhi style from Lucknow, or Awadh as it was earlier known. Until nearly the middle of the 20th century it was a princely state with Nawab rulers. Their feasts were renowned and even today the "dum pukht" technique, which literally means "to choke off the steam" is considered an important skill in any Awadhi chef's repertoire. One story says that 200 years ago, Nawab Asaf-ud-Daulah began the construction of a huge edifice, the Bara Imambara (which is the most important site in Lucknow today and is said to have the biggest vaulted hall in the world). He would destroy a part of the day's building work at night so that his workers would be in continuous employment. Food for the workers consisted of rice, meat, and vegetables and, as this was required day and night, it was put in a pot and sealed with dough to be slow-cooked all the time. One day, the Nawab tasted this meal, found it truly delicious and had it adopted into the royal kitchens. Awadh's most famous ruler, the artistic Wajid Ali Shah, is said to have refined the technique further. All sorts of fine dishes are made in the dum pukht style and specialty restaurants in many five star hotels around the country specialize in this cuisine.

delhi

New Delhi is the capital of India and has a cosmopolitan population of politicians, diplomats, and businessmen. The cuisine reflects the diversity of its people, and a variety of styles from the rich Punjabi to the vegetarian Bania and the nonvegetarian Kayastha coexist. The street corners are lined with stalls selling tandoori foods, crisp samosas, and syrupy sweets but, as evening turns to dusk and the street lights start to come on, the city's rich and famous dress up in their best silks to attend countless cocktail and dinner parties, often several in one night. At these, the food is a mix of world styles, each tempting the gourmet with newer and fancier creations.

Delhi is famous for its Mughlai cooking, a legacy left by the Mogul rulers who reigned from Delhi, their capital, over a large part of India, before the British took over. This cuisine is Muslim-influenced with several original names such as biryani, kabob, and kofta still in use. Mughlai cooking is truly fit for royalty with its buttery sauces, medley of vegetables, and rose-flavored sweets.

cauliflower and potatoes in spices
aloo gobi

This combination of cauliflower and potato is common all over India but, in the Punjab, it is quite a specialty, served with a roti (an unleavened bread) and a lentil dish. I like the cauliflower and the potatoes to turn slightly mushy, but you could cook the vegetables for a little less time and have them hold their shape if you prefer.

Serves: 4
Preparation time: 10 minutes
Cooking time: 25 minutes

3 tablespoons sunflower oil
1 medium onion, sliced
$^1/_2$ teaspoon ginger-garlic paste (page 11)
2 fresh small green chiles, chopped
1 cup peeled and cubed potatoes
$^2/_3$ cup fresh chopped tomatoes
6 ounces cauliflower, washed and
 cut into florets (about 2 cups)
$^1/_2$ teaspoon turmeric
1 teaspoon garam masala
Salt, to taste

1 Heat the oil in a kadhai or heavy pan. Add the onion and fry until soft. Add the ginger-garlic paste and fry for a few seconds. Add the chiles and the potatoes. Fry for a couple of minutes, stirring frequently to prevent the mixture from sticking. Add the tomatoes and let them soften.

2 Tip in the cauliflower, turmeric, garam masala, and salt. Mix well. Reduce the heat and cook, adding a few spoonfuls of water if it begins to stick to the pan. When the vegetables are completely done, in about 20 minutes, remove from the heat and serve hot.

spinach with cottage cheese
palak paneer

Indian cottage cheese is known as paneer. It is popular in the Punjab and is made at home by curdling whole milk and hanging up the milk solids in a piece of cheesecloth to drain off all the whey. The solid cheese is then pressed and cut into cubes. It is quite bland and will not keep for very long.

Commercially-available paneer is much denser than the homemade one because it is pressed under heavier weights. This dish can be found on the menu of most north Indian restaurants all over the world.

Serves: 4
Preparation time: 10 minutes
Cooking time: 25 minutes

18 ounces fresh spinach, washed and drained
3 tablespoons sunflower oil
$^1/_2$ teaspoon cumin seeds
6 ounces onions, grated (about 1 cup)
1 tablespoon ginger-garlic paste (page 11) –
 reserve some slivers of ginger for
 the garnish
2 large tomatoes, chopped
$^1/_2$ teaspoon chili powder
$^1/_2$ teaspoon garam masala
Salt, to taste
8 ounces paneer, cubed (about 2 cups)
2 tablespoons light cream

1 Put the spinach with some water in a heavy pan and cook, uncovered, over high heat until done, for about 5 minutes. Cool slightly and grind, along with enough of the cooking water, to a thick puree in a blender. Set it aside.

2 Heat the oil in a heavy pan and fry the cumin seeds until they turn dark. Add the onions and fry until soft.

3 Stir in the ginger-garlic paste and tomatoes and cook over low heat until mushy, for about 5 minutes.

4 Pour in the spinach puree, sprinkle in the chili powder, garam masala, and salt, and stir well. Bring to a boil. Reduce the heat and gently add the paneer. Simmer for 1 minute and remove from the heat. The paneer will soften in the heat.

5 Serve hot, swirled with the cream and sprinkled with slivers of ginger. This is great with a paratha (page 32) and some slices of fresh tomato, seasoned with salt and pepper.

potatoes in sour cream
banarasi aloo

spiced turnips
shalgam masala

Fennel seeds, used a lot in the cooking of Uttar Pradesh, add a sweet richness to curries and desserts, and a special zest to vegetables. They feature, powdered or whole, with a variety of vegetables and in a popular crisp, golden, fried dessert called "malpua," which is soaked in fennel-flavored sugar syrup. Fennel is also used in pickles and chutneys in north India, and a fennel infusion makes a delicious base for refreshing drinks. I love adding a few fennel seeds to my tea for a fuller flavor.

Serves: 4
Preparation time: 30 minutes
Cooking time: 15 minutes

3 tablespoons sunflower oil
1 teaspoon fennel seeds
10 ounces potatoes, boiled, peeled,
 and cubed (about 2 cups)
2 teaspoons tamarind pulp, diluted in a
 little water
1/4 cup tomato paste
1/2 teaspoon chili powder
1/2 teaspoon turmeric
1/2 teaspoon garam masala
Salt, to taste
1/4 cup light cream

1 Heat the oil in a wok or kadhai (or other heavy pan) and toss in the fennel seeds. When the seeds darken, add the potatoes and stir-fry for a few minutes. Add the tamarind pulp, tomato paste, spices, and salt, and stir until well blended. Cook over low heat until the potatoes are tender. Gently fold in the cream and heat through. The potatoes should be coated with a thick sauce. Serve hot.

Turnips are commonly used in the north either in stir-fries or in relishes. This pinkish white vegetable adds a crunch to many curries. I like it best when it gets slightly mushy as it seems to take on a creamy texture. Enjoy this with a hot roti (page 32).

Serves: 4
Preparation time: 15 minutes
Cooking time: 35 minutes

2 tablespoons sunflower oil
1 large onion, chopped
1 teaspoon ginger-garlic paste (page 11)
2 fresh small green chiles, chopped
2 medium tomatoes, chopped
1 teaspoon ground cumin
1 teaspoon ground coriander
1/2 teaspoon turmeric
Salt, to taste
10 ounces turnips, peeled and cubed
 (about 2 cups)
1 teaspoon jaggery or brown sugar
Finely chopped cilantro leaves for garnishing

1 Heat the oil in a kadhai or heavy pan and fry the onion until soft. Add the ginger-garlic paste and the chiles.

2 Add the tomatoes, the spices, and salt. Stir until well blended.

3 Mix in the turnips. Add about 2/3 cup of hot water and stir well.

4 Cover and bring to a boil, then reduce the heat and cook for about 20 minutes until the turnips are cooked.

5 Stir in the jaggery or sugar, lightly mashing the turnips as you go.

6 Garnish with the cilantro and serve the turnips piping hot.

kashmiri-style eggplant in yogurt
dahi baingan kashmiri

Serves: 4
Preparation time: 10 minutes
Cooking time: (approx.) 30 minutes

Sunflower oil for shallow frying
1 large eggplant, cut into thin discs
4 green cardamom pods, bruised
1/2 teaspoon ground fennel
1/2 teaspoon turmeric
1/2 teaspoon ground ginger
Pinch of asafetida
1 1/2 cups plain yogurt
Salt, to taste
Finely chopped cilantro leaves for garnishing

1 Heat the oil in a heavy, flat pan and, when very hot, shallow-fry the eggplant discs on both sides, until golden brown in color. Drain on paper towels and set aside. Discard all but 1 tablespoon of the oil from the pan.

2 Drop the green cardamom pods, the ground spices, and asafetida into the oil. Add the yogurt immediately as the spices will burn easily. Season with salt and heat through over low heat, stirring gently.

3 Add the fried eggplant discs and serve at once, garnished with the chopped cilantro. This goes well with Aloo Paratha (page 35).

silky eggplant mash with potatoes
baingan bharta

This most traditional dish is made by cooking the eggplant over an open flame so that it develops a smoky flavor. **This process can be done on the stovetop or in the oven. I have** modified the classic version of the recipe slightly to make it faster. This version does not have a smoky flavor but makes the most of the silky texture of the eggplant. The potatoes add a creaminess that goes well with the tomatoes and spices. I sometimes serve this as a topping for canapés or as a dip with cocktail snacks.

Serves: 4
Preparation time: 10 minutes
Cooking time: 40 minutes

1 large eggplant
2 tablespoons sunflower oil
1/2 teaspoon cumin seeds
1 medium onion, finely chopped
1 teaspoon ginger-garlic paste (page 11)
1 fresh small green chile, chopped
2 tablespoons tomato paste
1 teaspoon turmeric
1 teaspoon ground coriander
2 medium potatoes, peeled, boiled, and cubed
Salt, to taste
Chopped cilantro leaves for garnishing

1 Cut the eggplant into thick slices and place it in a heavy pan with enough water to cover the slices. Cover and cook for 12–15 minutes, reducing the heat when the water begins to boil.

2 Drain the eggplant. Mash the flesh and the skin of the eggplant with a fork. Set aside.

3 Heat the oil in a saucepan or wok and fry the cumin seeds until they change color, then add the onion and fry it until softened.

4 Add the ginger-garlic paste and the chile and fry for 1 minute. Then stir in the tomato paste and the remaining spices, and cook until well blended.

5 Season with salt and stir in the mashed eggplant. Mix well and fold in the potatoes before serving, sprinkled with the cilantro leaves and a wedge of lemon, if you like.

slow cooked mushrooms
dum ki khumb

Lucknow in the state of Uttar Pradesh is well known for its unique cuisine known as "Awadhi cooking" (page 21). Rich meat biryanis cooked in this style are very popular but there is also an amazing variety of vegetables such as baby corn, potatoes, and yams that are cooked in "dum." You will need a pan with a tight-fitting lid for this dish.

Serves: 4
Preparation time: 10 minutes
Cooking time: 30 minutes

1/2 teaspoon ginger-garlic paste (page 11)
1/4 teaspoon chili powder
10 ounces white mushrooms (about 3 cups), washed and drained
3 tablespoons ghee (you could use sunflower oil as a substitute)
1 large onion, sliced
1 teaspoon ground coriander
1 teaspoon ground fennel
3 tablespoons tomato paste
2 tablespoons ground almonds
Salt, to taste
1/2 cup plain yogurt
3 tablespoons condensed milk

1 Mix the ginger-garlic paste, chili powder, and mushrooms, and let them marinate while you prepare the onion.

2 Heat half the ghee or oil in a heavy pan and fry the onion until well browned. Whizz to a paste in a blender and set aside. In the same oil, fry the mushrooms for a few minutes, then drain and set aside.

3 Add the remaining ghee or oil to the pan and cook over medium heat, add the onion paste, remaining spices, and the tomato paste. Pour in a few tablespoons of water and stir to blend everything together.

4 Stir in the almonds, salt, yogurt, and condensed milk. Place the mushrooms in this "masala," stir, and cover with a tight-fitting lid.

5 Let the mushrooms cook in the steam for about 8 minutes and serve immediately with a roti or rice.

okra with tomatoes and green peppers
kadhai bhindi

Kadhai cooking (India's equivalent of a heavy wok) is a very popular north Indian style. Its close cousin is balti cooking, so popular in the UK. The recipe is cooked and served in the same pan, right from the fire to the table, so to speak.

When buying okra, make sure that you choose bright green ones. The freshest okra will snap when bent. If they double over, they are too old! Also, when cooking okra, make sure not to add any water to the pan. This makes the okra slimy. To get rid of the natural slime, add something acidic such as lemon juice.

Serves: 4
Preparation time: 10 minutes
Cooking time: 25 minutes

3 tablespoons sunflower oil
1 medium onion, sliced
1 medium green pepper, seeds removed
  and sliced
10 ounces okra (about 3 cups), washed,
  well-dried, tops removed, and cut in half
  lengthwise
2 ripe tomatoes, chopped
1 teaspoon turmeric
1/2 teaspoon chili powder
1/2 teaspoon garam masala
Salt, to taste
1 tablespoon lemon juice
Chopped cilantro leaves for garnishing

1 Heat the oil in a kadhai or heavy pan and fry the onion until soft.

2 Add the green pepper and continue to fry for a couple of minutes, then tip in the okra and stir well.

3 Add the tomatoes, spices, salt, and lemon juice, and mix well.

4 Let it cook over low heat, stirring frequently to keep the mixture from sticking, until the okra is tender. It will change from being slimy to quite firm.

5 Serve hot, sprinkled with the chopped cilantro leaves.

stuffed long chiles
bharwan mirch

There are many kinds of chiles and poblano (or long) chiles, made for stuffing. These are thick, long, and very bright green. They hold their shape well. Some can be very hot while others are quite mild. This dish is for those who like a bit of heat as it is quite a case of Russian Roulette here! For a milder version, try small green peppers instead.

Serves: 4
Preparation time: 10 minutes
Cooking time: 20 minutes

8 long poblano chiles
2 tablespoons sunflower oil
Large pinch of asafetida
2 cloves garlic, minced
1/4 cup chickpea flour
2 tablespoons ground cumin
2 tablespoons lemon juice
1/2 teaspoon turmeric
1/2 teaspoon chili powder
Salt
1 teaspoon cumin seeds

1 Slit the chiles lengthwise and carefully remove and discard all the seeds.

2 Heat 1 tablespoon of the oil in a pan and add the asafetida and garlic, then add the chickpea flour, ground cumin, lemon juice, turmeric, chili powder, and salt, and add a little water to make a thick paste. Cook for a couple of minutes then smear this paste on the inside of each chile.

3 Heat the remaining oil in a flat, nonstick pan until it is hot and add the cumin seeds. When they darken, arrange the chiles in the pan, slit-side up.

4 Cover the pan, lower the heat, and cook until the chiles are soft and slightly charred on the underside. Serve hot with rotis (page 32).

nine-jeweled curry
navratan korma

I have many good childhood memories associated with this dish. Growing up in Bombay, when going out to a restaurant was not such a commonplace thing as it is today, I would always order this dish. Its delightful combination of fruit and vegetables made all the more exciting with a few cherries and cream was for me, a dish made in heaven!

Serves: 4
Preparation time: 15 minutes
Cooking time: 25 minutes

10 ounces mixed vegetables—peas,
  cut-up carrots, chopped beans,
  and cubed potatoes (about 2 1/4-2 3/4 cups)
2 tablespoons sunflower oil
1 small onion, grated
1 tablespoon ginger-garlic paste (page 11)
3 tablespoons tomato paste
3 fresh small green chiles, slit down the middle
1 teaspoon turmeric
1 teaspoon garam masala
Salt
2 tablespoons cashews
2 tablespoons canned pineapple chunks,
  chopped
1/3 cup light cream
Few chopped candied cherries for garnishing
Cilantro leaves for garnishing
Grated cheddar cheese for garnishing

1 Prepare the vegetables by peeling and cutting up the carrots and potatoes, and finely chopping the beans. Boil all four vegetables in water until just tender, then drain and set aside.

2 Heat the oil in a large saucepan and fry the onion for a minute or so. Keep stirring to

prevent it from sticking and then stir in the ginger-garlic paste.

3 Add the tomato paste and chiles and cook until the oil separates, adding a couple of tablespoons of water to hasten the process.

4 Tip in the cooked vegetables, turmeric, garam masala, and salt. Mix gently and cook for a few minutes before folding in the cashews, pineapple, and cream. Heat through without letting it boiL

5 Serve hot, garnished with the cherries, cilantro leaves, and cheese.

everyday bread
roti/chapati

This is the most commonly made bread all over India. It is flaky and bland and makes a wonderful accompaniment to all the spice and herb flavors of the main dish. The art of making rotis is in getting the dough right and in the rolling out of perfectly round discs that are ready to roast. Many young girls in India, even as little as seven or eight, start out in the kitchen by helping their mothers to make rotis. My own daughter, who is seven, loves to make the balls of dough and has a great time rolling out what she calls "maps". We then eat up whole countries!

Serves: 4
Preparation time: 10 minutes
Cooking time: 20 minutes

1 pound whole wheat flour or atta
  (about 3¹/₂ cups)
2 teaspoons sunflower oil
Warm water as needed
Ghee or sunflower oil for brushing, if you like

1 Combine the flour and oil in a mixing bowl. Using your fingers, mix into a pliable dough with warm water. Knead for 5 minutes (the more you knead the dough, the softer the rotis).

2 Divide the dough into portions the size of a lime. Coat lightly with flour, shape into a ball in your palm, and flatten slightly.

3 Roll out into flat discs, 4 inches in diameter, flouring the board as necessary.

4 Heat a griddle or shallow pan. Cook the discs on the griddle until the surface appears bubbly. Turn over and press the edges down with a clean cloth to cook evenly. As soon as brown spots appear, the roti is done. Make sure that the roti is cooked evenly all over.

5 Remove and smear with ghee or oil, if using. Keep warm, enclosing in aluminum foil.

6 Cook all the rotis in the same way. Serve warm or, if serving later on, reheat them for a minute or so in a microwave or re-roast them on a skillet just enough to reheat them.

garlic bread
lahsun parathas

A meal in a north Indian home will always have some form of fresh bread, and there is an enormous array of different breads including those that are stuffed, layered, or flavored. This bread is strongly flavored and will go with a mild yogurt curry such as Kashmiri-style Eggplants in Yogurt (page 27). You could easily substitute the garlic with half a teaspoonful of cumin seeds for a milder bread.

Serves: 4
Preparation time: 15 minutes
Cooking time: 30 minutes

1 pound whole wheat flour or atta
  (about 3¹/₂ cups)
Water, as needed
2 tablespoons melted ghee or sunflower oil
1 teaspoon finely crushed garlic
1 teaspoon finely chopped cilantro leaves
¹/₄ teaspoon turmeric
Salt, to taste

1 Mix all the ingredients, reserving a little flour for dusting and rolling the bread, and knead to form a soft dough.

2 Divide the dough into 8 equal-sized balls. Roll each ball into a flat disc about 3¼ inches in diameter.

3 Smear each one with a little ghee or oil and roll into a hollow cylindrical or tube shape, then flatten with your palm, dust with a little flour, and roll out again to the same size.

4 Heat a griddle or frying pan and place one of the parathas on it. As soon as tiny bubbles appear on the surface, turn it over. Press down the edges with a clean cloth to ensure even cooking.

5 When the paratha is done, it should appear slightly puffed with brown patches. Remove it from the pan and keep warm in aluminum foil. Cook the remaining parathas in the same way. Serve hot.

fluffy, soft bread
bhatura

Chole-bhatura is a classic Punjabi combination of chickpeas served with fluffy, fried bread. It is as natural to eat this in a gourmet restaurant as it is to eat it at a roadside stall in any city of India. This combination is served as a complete meal accompanied only by an onion salad and a wedge of lemon.

Serves: 4
Preparation time: 15 minutes
Cooking time: 30 minutes

1 pound white flour (about 3^1/$_2$ cups)
^{3}/$_4$ cup plain yogurt
^{1}/$_2$ teaspoon baking powder
Sunflower oil for deep-frying

1 Reserve a little flour for dusting, and combine the rest with the yogurt and baking powder, and knead together with enough warm water to form a soft dough. Cover with a damp cloth and set aside for 30 minutes.

2 Divide the dough into small balls the size of a lime. Dust the counter with flour and roll out each bhatura into a disc 3^1/$_4$ inches in diameter.

3 Heat enough sunflower oil in a kadhai or deep frying pan. When it is smoking hot, reduce the heat and fry the bhaturas, one at a time, on each side, until fluffy. Serve hot with Chole (page 43).

potato-stuffed bread
aloo paratha

Breads made with a variety of stuffings are Punjabi specialties. Stuffings can be sweet or savory but spiced potatoes, cauliflower, turnips, and daikon are firm favorites. In many parts of the Punjab, this dish is eaten at any meal in the day. It goes well with a bowl of plain yogurt and some hot mango relish.

Serves: 4
Preparation time: 20 minutes
Cooking time: 45 minutes

For the stuffing:
2 medium baking potatoes, peeled and cubed
1 tablespoon sunflower oil
^{1}/$_2$ teaspoon cumin seeds
2 fresh small green chiles, finely chopped
^{1}/$_2$ teaspoon turmeric
Salt, to taste
2 tablespoons finely chopped cilantro leaves

For the bread:
1 pound whole wheat flour (about 3^1/$_2$ cups)
6 tablespoons sunflower oil
Salt, to taste
Water, as needed

1 To make the stuffing, boil the potatoes in a large pan of salted water until tender, drain them, then mash, and set aside.

2 Heat the sunflower oil and fry the cumin seeds until dark. Add the chiles, turmeric, and salt to taste.

3 Mix in the mashed potato and cilantro leaves and set aside.

4 To make the bread, combine the flour (reserving some for rolling) with 2 tablespoons of the oil, and the salt and water. Knead the dough until smooth and firm.

5 Divide the dough into 16 equal-sized balls. Roll each one out, dusting with a little flour if sticky, into a flat round about 3 inches in diameter.

6 Smear a layer of the potato mixture over one disc then place another rolled out disc of dough over this. Seal the edges to make a potato parcel. Make the other seven parathas.

7 Heat a frying pan and dot with oil. Cook the paratha until tiny, dark spots appear on the underside. Turn over and cook the other side. Keep warm in aluminum foil while you cook the rest of the parathas in the same way.

fragrant rice with red kidney beans
rajma pulao

Red kidney beans grow plentifully in north India. The area around the Vaishno Devi temple in Kashmir is famous for its rajma or red kidney bean curry, and weary travelers who walk long distances to seek the blessings of the Goddess are offered this wholesome meal at every eatery. A combination of rice and beans, it goes well with Navratan Korma (pages 30–31).

Serves: 4
Preparation time: 10 minutes
Cooking time: 30 minutes

3 tablespoons sunflower oil
4 green cardamom pods
6 cloves
8 black peppercorns
2 bay leaves
1¹/₂ cups basmati rice, washed and drained
Salt, to taste
3 tablespoons canned red kidney beans, drained
1 large onion, finely sliced

1 Heat 2 tablespoons of the oil in a heavy pan and fry the whole spices and the bay leaves for a couple of minutes until you get a wonderful aroma. Add the rice and fry for 2–3 minutes until shiny, stirring all the time to prevent burning.

2 Pour in 3 cups of hot water and season lightly with salt. Bring to a boil, reduce the heat, stir the rice once, and cover. Simmer for 10 minutes, remove from the heat, and leave the pan covered for another 5 minutes for the rice to finish cooking in the steam.

3 Uncover the pan and gently mix in the red kidney beans.

4 Heat the remaining oil in another pan and fry the onion over medium heat until golden brown in color. Drain and toss it over the pulao. Serve hot.

cumin-flavored rice
jeera pulao

Most Punjabi feasts will feature this rice simply because it goes so well with the spicy curries and lentil dishes of the region. The cumin adds a warm fragrance to the rice. There are two main varieties of cumin used in Indian cooking—one is called "jeera" and is quite strong, and the other, black cumin, is known as "shahijeera" and has a more delicate taste. You can use either variety in this recipe.

Serves: 4
Preparation time: 10 minutes
Cooking time: 20 minutes

1 tablespoon sunflower oil
1 teaspoon cumin seeds
1¹/₂ cups basmati rice, washed and drained
Pinch of salt

1 Heat the oil in a heavy pan and add the cumin seeds. When they turn dark, add the rice and fry until it is shiny; this takes about 3 minutes.

2 Add the salt and 3 cups of hot water and bring to a boil. Stir once, reduce the heat, cover, and cook for 10 minutes. Turn off the heat and leave the pan covered for another 5 minutes, so that the rice finishes cooking in the steam.

3 Uncover the pan and lightly run a fork through the rice to fluff it. Serve hot.

tomato-flavored rice
tamater pulao

I love to serve this rice at parties because it is so vibrant and delicious! The orange color complements most dishes and the tang of the tomatoes seems to add to the curry with which it is served. I always blanch the tomatoes because I don't like the skin interfering with the texture. To do this, simply nick the skins of the tomatoes with a sharp knife and immerse them for 1 minute or so in boiling water; the skins will then slip off easily.

Serves: 4
Preparation time: 10 minutes
Cooking time: 25 minutes

2 tablespoons sunflower oil
1 teaspoon cumin seeds
10 black peppercorns
1¹/₂ cups basmati rice, washed and drained
2 ripe tomatoes, peeled and chopped
2 tablespoons tomato paste
Salt, to taste
Fresh cilantro sprigs

1 Heat the oil in a heavy pan. Add the cumin seeds and peppercorns. Then add the rice and stir-fry until the rice grains turn shiny, for about 2–3 minutes.

2 Stir in the tomatoes, tomato paste, and salt. Mix well and pour in 3 cups of hot water. Bring to a boil.

3 Give it a good stir, reduce the heat and cover. Cook for 10 minutes until the rice is fluffy and dry. Turn off the heat and keep the pan covered for another 5 minutes.

4 Lift the lid and run a fork through the rice to loosen it. Serve hot, decorated with the cilantro.

rice cooked with garden vegetables, spices, and nuts
vegetable dum biryani

The word biryani is derived from the Farsi word "birian", which means fried before cooking. It is thought to have originated in Persia and could have come into north India via Afghanistan. As the Mughals spread their empire, the biryani traveled to various parts of the country so that today, a south Indian version also exists. A good biryani must have an amazing aroma, should not be too spicy, and, above all, the grains of rice must be loose and chewy. It is traditionally made in an earthenware pot and slow cooked to seal in the flavors. Make this as a special treat when you can spend a whole morning in the kitchen. Well worth it!

Serves: 4
Preparation time: 15 minutes
Cooking time: 1¹/₂ hours

Bouquet garni of 10 green cardamom pods,
  5 black cardamom pods, 12 black
  peppercorns, small stick of cinnamon,
  10 cloves, a few shavings of nutmeg,
  1 teaspoon fennel seeds,
  3 bay leaves
¹/₄ cup milk
Large pinch of saffron
¹/₄ cup rose water
3 tablespoons ghee
3 medium onions, sliced
1 tablespoon ginger-garlic paste (page 11)
2 tablespoons tomato paste
¹/₂ teaspoon turmeric
¹/₂ teaspoon garam masala
Salt, to taste
10 ounces mixed vegetables—carrots, peas,
  potatoes (about 2¹/₄–2³/₄ cups), peeled,
  cubed and boiled
1¹/₂ cups basmati rice
Handful of mint leaves, chopped
Handful of cilantro leaves, chopped
3 tablespoons slivered almonds

1 Preheat the oven to 425°F.

2 Put the spices (except 5 of the green cardamom pods) for the bouquet garni into a pan along with 3 cups of hot water and bring to a boil. Turn off the heat, cover the pan, and let it infuse into a savory aromatic liquid.

3 Crush the reserved green cardamoms finely in a mortar and mix with the milk, saffron, and rose water. Set aside. This is the sweet aromatic liquid.

4 Heat 1 tablespoon of the ghee in a pan and fry the onions over a medium heat until brown.

Remove half of them and reserve for the garnish. Add the ginger-garlic paste to the rest of the onions and stir for a couple of minutes. Whizz the mixture in a blender until smooth.

5 Heat another tablespoon of the ghee in a heavy pan and fry the onion mixture over high heat. Add the tomato paste and ground spices. Season with salt.

6 Drain the vegetables and add to the pan. Mix well and simmer for a few minutes until the ghee begins to separate. Remove from the heat and set aside.

7 Heat the remaining tablespoon of ghee in a separate pan and fry the rice over high heat. (Don't wash the rice beforehand.) In a few minutes, when it is shiny, strain half the savory liquid into the pan. Bring to a boil, reduce the heat, cover, and cook for about 6 minutes until the liquid has evaporated.

8 It's time to assemble the dish. The bottom and top layers are always rice. Put a layer of rice at the bottom of an ovenproof dish. Sprinkle some of the remaining savory liquid over it and some of the sweet liquid. Top with a layer of the vegetable curry. Sprinkle some of the fried onions, mint leaves, and cilantro leaves over it. Repeat with another layer of rice. Dot the almonds on top. Keep going until everything is used up and the top layer is rice. Seal the dish with aluminum foil.

9 Cook the biryani for 40 minutes in the oven, reducing the heat to 375°F after 20 minutes. Open the dish just before serving to release a burst of fragrance!

yellow lentils with onion and garlic
tarka dal

This is a very popular dish in north Indian restaurants around the world. The smooth creaminess goes well with rice or rotis, and the flavors of the spices seem to give an extra kick. I make my garam masala just before adding it to the dal as the flavor is strongest when fresh (page 58). Any leftovers can be mixed into whole wheat flour to make some dal roti, a bread that is as tasty as it is nutritious and comforting.

Serves: 4
Preparation time: 15 minutes
Cooking time: 15 minutes

1¹/₂ cups yellow lentils (dal)
2 tablespoons sunflower oil
1 teaspoon cumin seeds
1 large onion, sliced
1 tablespoon tomato paste
1 teaspoon ginger-garlic paste (page 11)
2 fresh small green chiles, slit
1 teaspoon turmeric
Salt, to taste
Handful of cilantro leaves, chopped
1 teaspoon garam masala

1 Pour boiling water over the lentils in a heavy pan and cook over medium heat for 30 minutes.

2 Heat the oil in another pan and add the cumin seeds. As they begin to crackle, add the onion and stir until golden and slightly crisp. Remove half the onion with a slotted spoon and drain on absorbent paper.

3 Add the tomato paste, ginger-garlic paste, chiles, and salt to the pan and cook until all are well blended.

4 Carefully pour the onion mixture over the cooked lentils and adjust the seasoning. Mix well. Serve hot with the reserved fried onions piled on top and a sprinkling of cilantro and garam masala.

black lentils cooked in butter and cream
dal bukhara

This dal is the defining lentil dish of the north, also called "kali dal." These lentils are made creamy and delicious with the addition of cream and butter (use sunflower oil for a lighter version), but the dal then becomes quite heavy to digest so it is well spiced. In India, it is cooked overnight over a low heat making the lentils silkier. Serve with plain boiled rice and a fresh green salad.

Serves: 4
Preparation time: 15 minutes + overnight soaking
Cooking time: 1¹/₄ hours

3 tablespoons ghee, butter, or sunflower oil
1 large onion, finely chopped
1 tablespoon ginger-garlic paste (page 11)
Large pinch of asafetida
1 teaspoon turmeric
1 teaspoon chili powder
1 teaspoon garam masala
2 large tomatoes, chopped
³/₄ cup black lentils, soaked overnight
Salt, to taste
¹/₄ cup heavy double cream
2 tablespoons chopped cilantro leaves

1 Heat the butter or oil in a large pan and fry the onion until golden. Add ginger-garlic paste and asafetida. Stir in the spices and tomatoes and cook for a few minutes to blend.

2 Drain the lentils and add them to the pan along with some salt. Pour in 1¹/₄ cups of hot water and bring to a boil. Reduce the heat and simmer for 1 hour until the lentils are cooked. Remove from the heat, stir in the cream, and serve, garnished with the cilantro leaves.

stir-fried black-eyed peas
bhuna lobhia

Black-eyed peas are beautifully silky and work very well with tomatoes and onions. They are rich in soluble fiber, which helps to eliminate cholesterol from the body. Most dried beans need overnight soaking but, if you are using cooked beans from a can, make sure you rinse them well to get rid of the salted water in which they are preserved.

Serves: 4
Preparation time: 15 minutes + overnight soaking
Cooking time: 20–30 minutes

2 tablespoons sunflower oil
1 teaspoon cumin seeds
Large pinch of asafetida
1 medium onion, finely sliced
1 tablespoon ginger-garlic paste (page 11)
1 cup black-eyed peas, soaked overnight and drained
1/2 teaspoon chili powder
1/2 teaspoon turmeric
2 large, ripe tomatoes, chopped
1 teaspoon garam masala
1/2 teaspoon sugar
Salt, to taste
Chopped cilantro leaves for garnishing

1 Heat the oil over a medium heat in a heavy saucepan or kadhai. Add the cumin seeds, fry until dark, and then add the asafetida and the onion and stir-fry until golden. Stir in the ginger-garlic paste and mix well.

2 Tip in the soaked beans, sprinkle in the chili powder and turmeric, and fry for 1 minute, before adding the tomatoes, garam masala, sugar, and salt. Mix, add a little water, cover, and bring to a boil. Reduce the heat and simmer until done. The beans should retain their shape. Mash a few to add thickness to the sauce.

3 Serve hot, garnished with the cilantro.

spiced chickpeas
chole

When I was a child, a dish of chole on the table meant that my mother had soaked the peas overnight and then boiled them for a long time to get them to the right texture. Happily today canned chickpeas are available everywhere, making this dish a breeze. Chole is a classic dish combined with Bhatura (page 35). The pomegranate seeds add a slight tang to the dish. If you cannot find them or the mango powder, substitute with 3 tablespoons of lemon juice.

Serves: 4
Preparation time: 15 minutes
Cooking time: 35 minutes

$1^1/_2$ **tablespoons dried pomegranate seeds (anardana), crushed**
1 teaspoon cumin seeds
2 tablespoons ghee or sunflower oil
2 x 15-ounce cans chickpeas, drained
1 teaspoon mango powder (amchoor)
$^1/_2$ teaspoon red chili powder
Salt, to taste
2 large onions, chopped
2 fresh small green chiles, sliced
$1^1/_4$-inch piece of ginger, cut into matchsticks
2 large tomatoes, chopped
Chopped cilantro leaves for garnishing

1 Heat a small frying pan and dry-roast the pomegranate and cumin seeds over a high heat until the seeds turn dark. Grind to a powder in a mortar and set aside.

2 Heat the ghee or oil in a heavy pan. Add the chickpeas and the reserved spice powder. Mix well. Add the mango powder, chili powder, and salt.

3 Add the chopped onions, green chiles, and about $^2/_3$ cup of hot water. Bring to a boil, reduce the heat, and cook over a low heat until the chickpeas are nearly dry.

4 Garnish with the ginger, chopped tomatoes, and cilantro leaves. Serve hot.

sour lentils flavored with garlic
khatti dal

Recipes for sour lentils can be found in every region of India. This recipe is from Lucknow in Uttar Pradesh known for the Awadhi style of cooking. Traditionally, in the days of the nawabs, this was done by highly skilled chefs called "rakabdars" who would only cook for a few people at a time. This was because presentation was as important as taste. Even today, the "rakabdars" that remain are considered artists rather than chefs and are very highly respected for their skill.

Serves: 4
Preparation time: 10 minutes
Cooking time: 45 minutes

1 1/2 cups yellow split lentils (toor dal),
   washed and drained
1/2 teaspoon turmeric
1 tablespoon tamarind concentrate
Salt, to taste
2 tablespoons ghee or sunflower oil
1 teaspoon cumin seeds
Large pinch of asafetida
3 dried red chiles, broken in half
3 cloves garlic, chopped
Chopped cilantro for garnishing

soy nuggets in tomato sauce
soya ki subzi

Soy beans grow widely in India and, for a large part of the vegetarian population, provide the protein content in a meal along with the staple dal. Soy protein is available as dried chunks or nuggets which soften on cooking. Their consistency is a bit like that of meat but the taste is blander. This curry goes well with a roti and salad.

Serves: 4
Preparation time: 10 minutes
Cooking time: 30 minutes

11 ounces soy nuggets or tofu cubes
  (2¹/₂–3 cups)
3 tablespoons sunflower oil
2 medium onions, chopped
1 tablespoon ginger-garlic paste (page 11)
2 ripe tomatoes
1 teaspoon cumin seeds
¹/₂ teaspoon turmeric
¹/₂ teaspoon chili powder
¹/₂ teaspoon garam masala
Salt, to taste
Chopped cilantro leaves for garnishing

1 Put the lentils and turmeric along with 3 cups of hot water in a saucepan and bring to a boil. Reduce the heat and simmer, partially covered, for about 30 minutes until the lentils are soft. If they dry out during the cooking, add a little more water until you get a mushy consistency.

2 Add the tamarind and salt and cook for a couple of minutes. Remove from the heat and set aside.

3 Heat the ghee or oil in a small saucepan and add the cumin seeds and asafetida. When the cumin turns dark, add the red chiles and garlic. Fry over a low heat until the garlic is golden brown. Garlic burns easily so quickly pour this mixture over the dal.

4 Serve hot, garnished with the cilantro.

1 Soak the soy nuggets in plenty of water and continue with the next steps.

2 Heat 2 tablespoons of the sunflower oil in a heavy pan and fry the onions until soft. Add the ginger-garlic paste and tomatoes, and cook until well blended. Remove from the heat and whizz in a blender until very smooth.

3 Heat the remaining oil in another pan and fry the cumin seeds until they darken. Add the onion and tomato mixture and fry for a few minutes.

4 Tip in the spices and salt. Squeeze the soy nuggets firmly to remove excess water and add them (or the tofu) to the pan. Stir in about ¹/₃ cup of water. Bring to a boil, reduce the heat, and simmer for about 5 minutes for the soy or tofu to soak up the spices. This dish should be semi-dry and served hot, sprinkled with the cilantro.

indian cottage cheese with peas
muttar paneer

In Delhi, no feast is complete without the inclusion of a dish made with paneer. Milk is available in plenty in the north, unlike in some of the drier regions of India, and most households will make this rather bland but wonderfully soft cheese at home. It is often combined with vegetables such as green peppers and mushrooms. The fenugreek in this recipe is available in Indian grocery stores as dried leaves with a wonderful fragrance. If you can't find it, substitute with the same quantity of ginger-garlic paste.

Serves: 4
Preparation time: 5 minutes
Cooking time: 20 minutes

3 tablespoons sunflower oil
1 teaspoon cumin seeds
$^1/_2$ teaspoon dried fenugreek leaves
1 large fresh green chile, slit
2 cups green garden peas
$^1/_2$ teaspoon turmeric
1 teaspoon ground coriander
Salt, to taste
Pinch of sugar
4 ounces paneer (about 1 cup)
Handful of cilantro leaves, chopped
Lemon juice

1 Heat the oil in a heavy pan and fry the cumin seeds until they darken slightly. Crumble in the fenugreek leaves and stir well.

2 Add the chile and the peas, along with the spices, salt, and sugar. Pour in about $^1/_3$ cup of water and cook until the peas are just tender, about 10 minutes. Add more water if necessary.

3 Fold in the paneer and simmer for a few minutes. Serve hot, and sprinkle with the cilantro and lemon juice.

indian cottage cheese with green peppers, onions, and tomatoes
paneer jalfrezi

Jalfrezi is a dish cooked with peppers and onions and has become one of the most popular Indian recipes in the world. I love the combination of crunchy onions and peppers, creamy paneer, and mushy tomatoes that come together with the spices. Serve this with a hot roti and nothing else.

Serves: 4
Preparation time: 15 minutes
Cooking time: 25 minutes

2 tablespoons sunflower oil
1 teaspoon cumin seeds
1 large onion, finely sliced
1 tablespoon ginger-garlic paste (page 11)
$^1/_2$ teaspoon turmeric
$^1/_2$ teaspoon chili powder
$^1/_2$ teaspoon ground coriander
Salt, to taste
5 ounces green peppers, sliced (about 2 cups)
2 ripe tomatoes, sliced
5 ounces paneer, cubed (about 1$^1/_4$ cups)
Chopped cilantro leaves for garnishing

1 Heat the oil in a heavy pan over a medium heat and fry the cumin seeds for 1 minute. Add the onion and fry until soft. Add the ginger-garlic paste and fry for a few seconds until well blended.

2 Sprinkle in the spices and cook over a low heat until the oil begins to separate, about 3 minutes. Stir frequently to prevent scorching.

3 Add the peppers, stir, and simmer gently until they are nearly done but still hold their shape, about 8 minutes.

4 Add the tomatoes and paneer and cook for a few minutes until soft but not mushy; the tomatoes will begin to soften at once because of the salt that has already been added.

5 Remove from the heat and serve hot, garnished with the cilantro leaves.

yogurt curry with fried dumplings
pakodewali kadhi

This is one of the most famous curries from the state of Uttar Pradesh. It is served with rice and hot mango relish. The pakoras or dumplings that go into the curry can be flavored with a variety of vegetables such as cooked spinach, grated carrots, fenugreek leaves, or florets of cauliflower.

Serves: 4
Preparation time: 10 minutes
Cooking time: 30 minutes

1¹/₃ cups plain yogurt
1 cup chickpea flour (besan)
1 fresh small green chile, finely chopped
¹/₂ teaspoon turmeric
2 teaspoons sugar
Salt, to taste
2 tablespoons sunflower oil
1 teaspoon cumin seeds
10 black peppercorns
6 cloves
2 tablespoons ghee (optional)
¹/₂ teaspoon chili powder

For the dumplings:
1 cup chickpea flour (besan)
1 medium onion, finely chopped
Pinch of cumin seeds
Sunflower oil for deep-frying

1 Whisk the yogurt with the chickpea flour, green chile, turmeric, sugar, salt, and 1¹/₄ cups of cold water.

2 Heat the oil in a heavy pan and add the cumin seeds, peppercorns, and cloves.

3 Give the yogurt mixture a good blend, ensuring that there are no lumps left, and pour into the pan. Bring to a boil. Reduce the heat and cook, stirring frequently, until the consistency resembles that of a thick gravy and the raw flour aroma has gone. Remove from the heat.

4 For the dumplings, make a thick batter with the chickpea flour, onion, and cumin seeds and add water as necessary.

5 Heat the oil in a heavy pan. When it starts smoking, lower the heat and drop in 2–3 separate teaspoonfuls of batter at a time. Fry until golden, drain, and dip them into a bowl of water to soften a bit. Remove immediately, squeeze out the water, and add them to the yogurt curry. Make all the dumplings in this manner.

6 Heat the ghee (if using) in a small pan (you could use the hot sunflower oil instead) and add the chili powder. Pour this mixture over the curry at once and serve without stirring.

spicy paneer fritters
paneer pakoras

Pakoras, popular snacks or accompaniments not just in India but all over the world, are made with vegetables such as cauliflower, potatoes, and eggplant, held together with spiced chickpea flour. One of my most relaxing memories is of eating hot pakoras during the Bombay monsoons, a time when it rains in sheets and going out is impossible.

Serves: 4
Preparation time: 15 minutes
Cooking time: 30 minutes

For the batter:
1 cup chickpea flour (besan)
1 teaspoon chili powder
1 teaspoon ginger-garlic paste (page 11)
1/2 teaspoon cumin seeds
Handful of cilantro leaves, finely chopped
Large pinch of baking soda
Salt, to taste

Sunflower oil for deep-frying
10 ounces paneer, cut into strips
  (about 2 1/2–3 cups)

1 Mix all the batter ingredients with enough water to make a thick batter. Heat the oil in a deep kadhai or frying pan until it smokes. Dip each strip of paneer into the batter and gently add to the hot oil. Reduce the heat for the pakora to cook through. Fry until golden, then drain on absorbent paper. Fry 2–3 pakoras at a time, regulating the heat to ensure even cooking.

2 Serve hot with ketchup and a tablespoon of bottled mint sauce stirred into about 5 tablespoons of plain yogurt.

tiny chickpea flour balls in yogurt
boondi raita

This is probably the most popular raita made in north Indian homes. Although ready-made boondi or flour balls are available in many places, it is easy to make your own. The procedure is a little messy but great fun and the kids can try if they are supervised by an adult. The semolina helps to make them crunchier. The boondis can be stored in an airtight container for a couple of months. They can also be sprinkled over rice or vegetable stir-fries to add crunch.

Serves: 4
Preparation time: 15 minutes
Cooking time: 25 minutes

For the boondi:
1 cup chickpea flour (besan)
1 tablespoon semolina
1/2 teaspoon salt

Sunflower oil for deep-frying

For the raita:
3/4 cup plain yogurt
Salt, to taste
Pinch of sugar
1/2 teaspoon cumin seeds

1 To make the boondi, combine the flour, semolina, salt, and 1/3 cup of cold water in a mixing bowl. Whisk together to remove any lumps.

2 Heat the oil in a kadhai or deep frying pan.

3 When it reaches smoking point, reduce the heat. Hold a perforated spoon (one with large holes) about 4 inches above the pan and pour some batter onto it. It should drip in droplets into the oil.

4 The drops of batter float up to the surface of the oil quite quickly. Fry for 1 minute or so, remove with a slotted spoon, and drain on absorbent paper. Fry the rest of the batter in the same way.

5 Make the raita by combining the yogurt, salt, and sugar in a serving bowl. Set aside.

6 Heat a small saucepan and dry-roast the cumin seeds until they turn dark. Then crush them to a fine powder in a mortar. Stir into the yogurt.

7 Just before serving, stir in some of the boondis to make a semi-liquid raita. The next time you make this dish, it will be a lot easier if you have some boondis left over!

onion and mint raita
dahi kuchumber

A raita is usually a yogurt-based salad and is almost always served with a north Indian meal. The name of this dish literally means yogurt salad. Mughlai food, with its rich sauces and creamy curries, is served with this fresh onion raita. I use Greek yogurt for a fuller flavor but do use low-fat yogurt if you prefer.

Serves: 4
Preparation time: 15 minutes
Cooking time: nil

3/4 cup plain Greek yogurt
Salt, to taste
1 fresh small green chile, very finely chopped
1 medium onion, finely chopped
Handful of mint leaves, washed and
 finely chopped

1 Beat the yogurt with the salt for 1 minute. Add the rest of the ingredients and serve

2 If preparing in advance, add the salt at the last minute.

sweet star fruit preserve
karambal ka murabba

Preserve- and pickle-making are traditional skills passed down from mother to daughter. I remember my grandmother making a variety of mango preserves every summer—hot, sweet, and salty. I especially loved her raw mangoes in brine which would keep for a whole year. This star fruit preserve can be stored for about a month in the fridge.

Serves: 4
Preparation time: 5 minutes
Cooking time: 30 minutes

2 large juicy star fruits (carambola), sliced
1/2 cup sugar
Juice of 1 lemon
Pinch of saffron strands

1 Put the star fruit with half the sugar in a heavy pan. Pour in 2/3 cup of water and bring to a boil. Reduce the heat and simmer for 5 minutes until the fruit is tender but holds its shape. Strain the fruit out of the syrup and set aside.

2 Add the remaining sugar to the cooking liquor in the pan and cook until it becomes a syrup of single thread consistency. Test this by putting a drop of syrup on a cold plate and dabbing it with your finger—it should feel sticky and thick.

3 Add the lemon juice, saffron, and cooked fruit to the syrup and simmer for 1 minute. Remove from the heat, cool completely, and store in a clean, airtight glass jar in the fridge.

sweet potato kabobs
shakarkand ke kebab

I remember as a teenager in Bombay going to a friend's farm for a sleepover and having the most delicious farm meal. Her dad cooked us some meat on a barbeque and then he had a hole dug in the ground, put the live coals from the barbeque into it, and placed some sweet potatoes and onions in their skins on top. He covered this with some stones and in a while we had charred vegetables that we peeled and ate with the meat. Fabulous and fun! Commercially made paneer has been pressed to make it hard and therefore to grate.

Serves: 4
Preparation time: 15 minutes
Cooking time: 40 minutes

¹/₄ cup cashews
³/₄ cup chickpea flour (besan)
10 ounces sweet potatoes, boiled, peeled, and grated (about 1¹/₃ cups)
4 ounces paneer, grated (about 1 cup)
1 tablespoon peeled and grated fresh ginger
Small handful of mint leaves, chopped
Few shavings of nutmeg
Salt and pepper, to taste
Lemon juice to drizzle on top

Wooden skewers

1 Dry-roast the cashews in a small pan. When they turn golden, remove and set aside.
In the same pan, dry-roast the chickpea flour. Keep stirring to prevent it from sticking. When the raw aroma has transformed into a cooked aroma, in about 6–7 minutes, remove and set aside.

2 Preheat the oven to 425°F. Combine the sweet potatoes, paneer, ginger, mint leaves, nutmeg, cashews, and the salt and pepper.

3 Add the roasted chickpea flour and kne well with your fingers until a dough is for

4 Divide the dough into 8 portions and s around wooden skewers.

5 Reduce the oven temperature to 350°F Place the skewers on a lined baking tray bake for 20 minutes until golden. Serve drizzled with the lemon juice.

otatoes and green ea samosas

utter ke samose

nosas are very popular all over the world
can be served as a snack, a main meal, or
cnic treat. In India, they are served with
chup, sweet and sour tamarind chutney, or
icy mint relish. The potatoes in this
pe need to be cut up finely, almost the
of a fingernail. They should retain their
pe but melt in the mouth. Although they
traditionally deep-fried, I bake my
osas as a healthier option.

es: 4 (makes 12 samosas)
aration time: 15 minutes
king time: 1 hour

blespoons sunflower oil
aspoon cumin seeds
aspoon turmeric
aspoon chili powder
spoon ground coriander
unces potatoes, peeled, cut into small
es, boiled, and drained
nces frozen green peas, cooked
drained
to taste
nces frozen ready-to-use phyllo pastry
gh (about 1¹/₄ cups)

1 Heat the oil in a heavy pan and fry the
cumin seeds for a few seconds, until they turn
dark. Reduce the heat.

2 Add the spices and stir in the potatoes at
once as the spices will scorch easily. Add the
peas and salt and cook for a few minutes,
until well blended.

3 Line a baking tray with aluminum foil and
preheat the oven to 425°F.

4 Lay a sheet of phyllo dough on a flat
surface. Fill with a bit of the potato and pea
mixture. Fold the pastry dough to make a
triangle and continue similarly for the rest of
the filling. (Folding technique: lift the top left
corner and fold it over the filling to be in line
with the bottom edge, making a triangle
shape. Now lift the right bottom corner over
to the top and then the top left corner down
again. Continue until you have a triangular
package.)

5 Bake in the oven for 25–30 minutes,
turning over once so both sides cook.
Serve hot.

carrot halwa
gajar ka halwa

This is a winter favorite in north India as its carotene content helps to protect against the harmful pollution that lingers in the cold, heavy air. Winter carrots grown in India are bright red giving this dish its unique jeweled color. Serve it all through the year; in the summer, serve it warm with vanilla ice cream and in the winter, with a dash of cream.

Serves: 4
Preparation time: 15 minutes
Cooking time: 40 minutes

$1/2$ cup sugar
2 tablespoons ghee
10 ounces carrots, grated (about $2^{1}/4$ cups)
$1^{1}/4$ cup whole milk
$1/2$ teaspoon ground cardamom
1 tablespoon finely chopped cashews

1 Mix the sugar with 1 cup of water in a heavy saucepan and bring to a boil. Reduce the heat and cook until the syrup has thickened slightly. Remove from the heat and set aside.

2 In the meantime, heat the ghee in a heavy pan and fry the carrots, stirring occasionally to prevent them from sticking. When they turn translucent, add the sugar syrup and stir until blended.

3 Pour in the milk, reduce the heat, and cook until the carrots are mushy and the milk has been soaked up. The ghee should begin to separate at this point.

4 Remove from the heat, mix in the cardamom, and serve warm, decorated with the nuts.

crisp toast in nutty saffron milk
shahi tukre

This classic dessert was created for the Mogul rulers a few centuries ago and is still served at feasts and banquets. As a child, I remember my mother making it for Sunday lunch and it was always a firm favorite! Although the toast needs to be crisp, I quite like it soft and chewy, full of the sweet saffron milk that envelops it.

Serves: 4
Preparation time: 10 minutes
Cooking time: 30 minutes

Sunflower oil for deep-frying
4 slices of white bread, each cut into
  4 squares
$2/3$ cup whole milk
$2/3$ cup evaporated milk
$1/2$ cup condensed milk
Sugar, to taste
Generous pinch of saffron
2 tablespoons crushed pistachios

1 Heat the oil and fry the squares of bread on both sides until golden. Lift from the pan and drain on absorbent paper.

2 Mix all the milks, sugar, and saffron, and bring to a boil. Simmer for 10 minutes or so until the mixture thickens. Remove from the heat and let it cool.

3 To serve, put the fried bread toasts on a platter and sprinkle half the pistachios over them. Pour the saffron milk on top and decorate with the rest of the pistachios.

angoes with semolina
akaramba

ummer specialty in Lucknow and
rounding areas, this Awadhi dish makes
most of the seasonal fruit. The beauty of
adhi desserts lies in their charming
bination of Hindu and Muslim cultures so
t there is a place for wonderful Eid
serts such as sevaiyan and for traditional
ali desserts such as jalebis and laddoos. I
e sometimes made this with other fruit
h as strawberries and nectarines.

ves: 4
aration time: 10 minutes
king time: 25 minutes

blespoons ghee or butter
unces mangoes, peeled, pitted, and cut
o small chunks (about 1 cup)
blespoons sugar
oves
een cardamom pods, bruised
up semolina
up warm milk

1 Heat half the ghee or butter in a pan and sauté the mango for a few minutes until slightly mashed. Set aside.

2 Combine the sugar and 6 tablespoons of water in a small pan and bring to a boil. Reduce the heat and simmer for a few minutes until slightly thickened. Add the mango and cook for 1 minute, then set aside.

3 Heat the rest of the ghee in a heavy saucepan and fry the spices for 1 minute.

4 Add the semolina and fry, stirring constantly to prevent it from sticking. In about 5 minutes, add the milk and stir continuously to prevent lumps from forming, until the milk has been absorbed and the semolina is soft.

5 Pour in the mango mixture and serve warm.

indian rice pudding
chaaval ki kheer

Kheer is a generic term given to puddings that resemble creams. They can be made with nuts or fruit and always have a milk component. They are considered food for the gods: in fact the god Rama was thought to have been conceived after his mother ate some magical kheer. Rice kheer is made all over India and this is the northern version. In the south, cooks add slivers of coconut, or flavor the dish with edible camphor. Broken basmati rice is available commercially.

Serves: 4
Preparation time: 30 minutes
Cooking time: 1 hour

3/4 cup broken basmati rice (this gives a better, sticky texture to the pudding)
2 1/2 cups whole milk
1/4 cup ground almonds
2/3 cup evaporated milk
Sugar, to taste
2 tablespoons chopped pistachios
1/2 teaspoon ground cardamom

1 Bring the rice to a boil with the milk in a heavy pan, then let it simmer for 1 hour or until mushy. Mash the rice roughly with a whisk while still on the burner.

2 Blend the ground almonds into the evaporated milk and add to the rice. Stir until thick and creamy.

3 Add the sugar and pistachios. Sprinkle the ground cardamom over it and stir well. Serve chilled or warm, depending upon the weather; delicious warm on a winter's evening.

salted lassi with ginger
adrak ki lassi

This is a wonderful drink in the summer. Ayurveda, the Indian system of holistic health, suggests that ginger is good for stimulating the appetite, a much needed thing in the summer! It is also called "maha aushadhi" or great medicine because it has so many health properties. It is best to peel ginger lightly: the essential oil to which it owes its efficacy lies just beneath the skin.

Serves: 4
Preparation time: 10 minutes
Cooking time: nil

1 teaspoon cumin seeds, dry-toasted and crushed in a mortar
1¹/₄ cups cold water
1 cup plain yogurt
1 teaspoon finely grated fresh ginger
Salt, to taste

Combine all the ingredients, whisk well, and serve chilled.

raw mango cooler
panha

Serves: 4
Preparation time: 10 minutes
Cooking time: 30 minutes

1 raw green mango
¹/₂ cup sugar
Pinch of salt
Few strands of saffron
Couple of twists of the peppermill
Seeds from 3 green cardamom pods, crushed

1 Peel the mango and chop roughly, taking care to cut around the pit. Place the flesh in a pan with 1¹/₄ cups of water and bring to a boil. I always boil the mango pit for its flavor. Reduce the heat and simmer for 15 minutes until the mango is pulpy.

2 Remove from the heat, cool, and whizz in a blender until smooth. If the pulp is stringy or thick, strain it through a fine strainer.

3 Add the rest of the ingredients and return to the heat. Cook for a few minutes until the sugar has dissolved completely.

4 Cool and store the concentrate in the fridge. To make a glassful, pour in 2–3 tablespoons of the concentrate and top with chilled water.

garam masala

In the north, where the winters are bitterly cold, a blend called garam masala, meaning hot spice, is preferred to chiles to add heat to many dishes. Chiles cool the body by promoting perspiration whereas garam masala creates heat within the body, keeping it warm. Some of the most expensive spices go into the making of garam masala and there are as many recipes for it as there are households in India. Depending upon individual taste, the proportions of the various ingredients can be adjusted but every blend of garam masala has a rich, warm fragrance and tastes hot and aromatic.

Commercially produced garam masala is often sold in large quantities that cannot be used up quickly enough by most of us so I always make my own blend at home just when I need to use it. It takes a few minutes and the flavors are astounding. Here is my simplest recipe and it will make enough for one curry for four people.

10 black peppercorns
1 teaspoon cumin seeds
Small stick of cinnamon
Seeds from 2–3 green cardamom pods
3 cloves

Dry-roast all the spices in a small saucepan for a couple of minutes until a delicious fragrance wafts up. Put the spices in a mortar and crush to a fine powder, or blitz in a coffee grinder. Use at once.

the we

the states of western india

rajasthan

The west includes the states of Rajasthan, Gujarat, Maharashtra, and Madhya Pradesh. Within these states exist many communities such as the Bohri Muslims of Gujarat, the Parsees who live predominantly in Mumbai and Gujarat, and the Sindhis who have made Mumbai and Pune their home. Mumbai, the capital of the state of Maharashtra and the largest commercial city, has its own unique cuisine because it is home to every community of India. Mumbai street food is famous and it is common to see groups of people eating at little roadside carts all through the day.

Rajasthan, which lies in the Thar Desert is also called the Land of Princes because of the many princely kingdoms that existed here before Independence in 1947. In all the royal kitchens of Rajasthan, the preparation of food was raised to the levels of an art form. The Khansamas or royal cooks were artists who guarded their recipes with pride and passed them down only to a worthy successor. I have spoken to several who, when asked about a recipe, would smile and say something like, "Master liked my cooking."

The everyday Rajasthani cooking was designed for the war-like lifestyle of medieval Rajasthan when war lords spent many days away from home, in battle. Also, being an arid desert, the availability of ingredients of the region was relatively limited. Food that could remain unspoiled for several days and could be eaten without heating was preferred, more out of necessity than choice. The scarcity of water, fresh vegetables, and delicate spices has had its effect on the cooking of this state. Most foods are still cooked in ghee.

In the desert belt of Jaisalmer, Barmer, and Bikaner, chefs use less water and more milk, buttermilk, and ghee. A special feature of Maheshwari cooking is the use of amchoor or mango powder, making up for the scarcity of tomatoes in the desert, and asafetida, to flavor curries that do not have the luxury of onions and garlic. Generally, most bright red Rajasthani curries look spicier than they actually are and, if you travel through Rajasthan, you will see heaps of brilliant red chiles drying in the strong sunshine for use later on.

gujarat

Gujarat is the mango shaped state in the west of India. Its northern region is famous for a delicate, vegetarian cuisine and most especially for the thali, a metal plate with several small bowls filled with an array of tempting dishes. The thali has rice, breads, fried accompaniments called farsans, vegetables, lentils, and sweets all served at the same time.

Although Gujarat has had many foreign influences over the years, the basic cuisine has remained the same. Even within Gujarat, the cuisine is varied within the different areas. Some areas are drier than others. Kathiawari and Kachchi food both use red chili powder to create heat. In the southern part of the state, green chiles are used for the same purpose, most often in conjunction with fresh ginger. In Surat, sugar is added to many dishes, even lentils and vegetables, and much of the cuisine has a sweet, tangy flavor. The food of Surat is renowned all over India. Oondhiyoon, which is a delicious combination of winter vegetables, contains sweet, sharp, and herby flavors. The delicate balance of flavors—sweet, tangy, and sharp—is what makes the food of Surat unique.

Gujarat was also home to the Bohri Muslim community which migrated to Mumbai in large numbers. Their cooking is a mix of the local Gujarati with Islamic overtones and some of the delicacies such as lamba pau, a bread that is smoky from being baked in a wood oven, is found only in exclusive eateries today.

maharashtra

Maharashtra lies in the west of India and has a long coastline along the Arabian Sea. Many communities live here—different sects of Maharashtrians and the settlers who came from other states.

Native Maharashtrian cooking has many styles, the Pune Brahmin style with its sweet, simple flavorings and use of peanuts, the fiery curries of the Deccan Plateau, and the coconut and tamarind flavorings of the coastal areas. The state grows a large variety of crops such as peanuts, coconuts, rice, and mangoes. The most sought after mango in India, the Alphonso, is grown here in Ratnagiri.

The biggest city in the state is Mumbai. This cosmopolitan city is dotted with innumerable restaurants serving up every type of regional cuisine. The Parsees who came from Persia and settled in Gujarat later moved to Mumbai. Their cooking is a mix of Iranian and Hindu and, out of respect to the local community, they do not eat beef. Their cooking is exemplified by the sweet and sour dhansak, stews, and dessert custards.

The Sindhi community migrated from Pakistan and many of them set up homes in Mumbai. They are known for their love of food and their cooking is fresh and flavorful. Leafy vegetables imbued with cumin, fried breads, and spiced lentils with garlic are specialties. Their love of various poppadoms is legendary and they make them using anything from lentils to lotus root.

madhya pradesh

This state lies at the center of India and is often called her "heart." The cooking is influenced by all the surrounding states, most importantly by Gujarat and Maharashtra. MP, as it is known, has a great culture of hospitality and I have never been to any other place in the world where the people eat and offer others so much food. There seem to be six meals a day—breakfast, elevenses (mid-morning), lunch, tea (mid-afternoon), dinner, and supper (late-night) with many "munchings" in between!

Much of MP has Hindu cooking. Indore is famous for its pickle shops that sell preserved fruit and vegetables. I was once taken to a pickle shop that was heaven for a food enthusiast like me, every imaginable pickle made in the region filled rows and rows of clean glass jars. As I pointed out my choices, the vendor weighed and filled tiny plastic bags with flaming scarlet, golden yellow, or rich terracotta colored pickles. There were whole lemons with cloves and ginger, stuffed red chiles (surprisingly mild), and sliced green mango with fennel and mustard seeds at home for many months afterwards. In Indore, the local main street turns into a food lane called the sarafa after the stores close and every night people stroll along this road to eat fresh samosas, hot sweet jalebis, and to drink warm nut-flavored milk.

Bhopal, the capital, is an exception. Ruled for many years by a Muslim ruler, the cuisine is a mix of Islamic and Hindu styles. Kabobs and biryanis sit next to simple stir-fries and fresh breads. Desserts are much loved and tiny milk burfies and halwas are served at each meal.

gujarati-style cabbage and peas stir-fry
kobi vatana

Gujarati cooking is very delicate and this recipe works well if the cabbage is finely shredded. It should look translucent and shiny when served, and is best cooked with the pan uncovered as this helps get rid of the rather unpleasant smell. This slightly sweet stir-fry goes well with roti (page 32).

Serves: 4
Preparation time: 10 minutes
Cooking time: 25 minutes

2 fresh small green chiles, finely chopped
1 teaspoon grated, fresh ginger
2 tablespoons sunflower oil
1 teaspoon black mustard seeds
1/2 teaspoon cumin seeds
Pinch of asafetida
1 teaspoon turmeric
10 ounces cabbage, finely shredded
  (about 5 cups)
11/4 cups fresh or frozen peas
Salt, to taste
2 tablespoons freshly grated coconut

1 Crush the chiles and ginger to a paste in a mortar or coffee grinder (wash it after use).

2 Heat the oil in a wok or a heavy pan until almost smoking. Add the mustard seeds and let them pop. Add the cumin seeds, asafetida, and chile-ginger paste, and stir for a few seconds. Sprinkle in the turmeric and add the cabbage and peas. Season with salt and stir until the vegetables start to turn translucent. Pour in a few tablespoons of water. Reduce the heat and cook, adding a little more water as necessary, until the vegetables are al dente. Serve hot, sprinkled with the coconut.

eggplants and potatoes in peanut sauce
vengan bataka

I first tasted this in a friend's house in Mumbai and have always made it for special occasions since then. The ingredients list may seem a bit daunting, but the final dish is well worth it. Also, most of the ingredients are not too difficult to get hold of. Fenugreek leaves add a curry-like flavor and, if you are using them, pinch off the leaves and discard the stalks. Serve this with a roti or with poories (page 74).

Serves: 4
Preparation time: 15 minutes
Cooking time: 45 minutes

1 teaspoon white sesame seeds, toasted
2 teaspoons peanuts, toasted
2 tablespoons chickpea flour (besan)
141/2-ounce can chopped tomatoes
1 tablespoon ginger-garlic paste (page 11)
Handful of fenugreek leaves, chopped
  (optional)
Handful of cilantro leaves, chopped
1/2 teaspoon turmeric
1/2 teaspoon chili powder
Salt, to taste
1 teaspoon brown sugar
10 ounces small eggplants, slit down
  the middle but stalks left on
2 tablespoons sunflower oil
1/2 teaspoon black mustard seeds
1 small potato, peeled and quartered

1 Whizz the sesame seeds and peanuts in coffee grinder or crush them finely in a mo and set aside.

2 Heat a pan and dry-roast the chickpea fl stirring constantly for 2–3 minutes, and th mix well into the chopped tomatoes in a si bowl and set aside.

3 In a mixing bowl, combine the peanut mixture, tomato mixture, ginger-garlic pas and the chopped leaves. Add the spices a season with salt, then the sugar.

4 Stuff the eggplants with this mixture sa any that is left over to add to the pan later

5 Heat the oil in a heavy pan or kadhai. A the mustard seeds and let them pop.

6 Gently place the eggplants and potatoe the pan and pour in any leftover spice mi Pour in a few tablespoons of water and co the pan.

7 Bring to a boil, reduce the heat, and si until the vegetables are cooked, for about 25 minutes. Serve hot. The sauce should quite thick.

dilled vegetables
saibhaji

This is a Sindhi favorite of mine. The dish is creamy and nutritious and goes well with rotis. Dill leaves are popular among certain communities of India—the Sindhis and the Gujaratis to name two. Dill combines well with lentils and garlic to make an herby dal that is delicious with rice. Dill leaves are wispy and delicate and they cook fast. Their strong flavor is unpopular with some people but, in this dish, it seems to complement the spinach rather than overwhelm it.

Serves: 4
Preparation time: 20 minutes
Cooking time: 45 minutes

2 tablespoons sunflower oil
$1/2$ teaspoon cumin seeds
2 teaspoons ginger-garlic paste (page 11)
4 teaspoons split chickpea lentils
  (channa dal), washed and drained
$1^1/4$ pounds spinach, washed and chopped
Handful of dill leaves, chopped
2 medium tomatoes, chopped
1 small potato, peeled and chopped
2 small eggplants, chopped (or half a
  large one)
2 carrots, peeled and chopped
$1/2$ teaspoon chili powder
$1/2$ teaspoon turmeric
Salt, to taste

1 Heat the oil in a pan. Add the cumin seeds and as they begin to darken, in a minute or so, add the ginger-garlic paste.

2 Stir and add the lentils, spinach, dill, tomatoes, and vegetables. Mix in the chili, turmeric, and salt. Pour in about $2/3$ cup of water and simmer gently until the lentils are cooked, for about 35 minutes. The vegetables will be mushy by now.

3 Remove from the heat and whisk gently to blend into a smooth but thick consistency. Serve very hot.

green beans with mustard
farasbeechi bhaji

This stir-fry from Maharashtra is one my mother made quite often when I was a child. The beans must be chopped quite finely to get the best flavor. I find that the zing of mustard seeds and the bitter taste of cumin seeds complement this vegetable beautifully. Cooking without a lid on the pan keeps the beans green and fresh looking. I sometimes add a few tablespoons of canned black-eyed peas for a bit of variety.

Serves: 4
Preparation time: 5 minutes
Cooking time: 15 minutes

2 tablespoons sunflower oil
1 teaspoon black mustard seeds
$1/2$ teaspoon cumin seeds
1 medium onion, finely chopped
10 ounces green beans, finely chopped
  (about 2 cups)
Salt, to taste
1 tablespoon lemon juice
3 tablespoons dry, unsweetened coconut

1 Heat the oil and add in the mustard seeds. As they pop, add the cumin and onion. Stir and fry until the onion is soft.

2 Add the green beans and salt. Pour in a few tablespoons of water and cook uncovered until the beans are tender.

3 Remove from the heat, stir in the lemon juice, and serve hot, sprinkled with the coconut.

corn on the cob in coconut curry
bhajani makka

This recipe is from the coasts of Maharashtra, a region rich in coconut and native fruits such as mango and jackfruit. The basic curry paste in this recipe is very versatile and tastes better the next day. In its place of origin, it is used with a variety of vegetables such as cauliflower, potatoes, and peas. It has always proved a great hit at my parties.

Serves: 4
Preparation time: 15 minutes
Cooking time: 40 minutes

1¹/₄ pounds corn on the cob, cut into
 ³/₄-inch chunks
3 tablespoons sunflower oil
10 black peppercorns
³/₄-inch stick of cinnamon
6 cloves
2 teaspoons coriander seeds
1 large onion, finely sliced
5 ounces freshly grated or dried coconut
1 teaspoon cumin seeds
1 medium tomato, chopped
1 teaspoon chili powder
1 teaspoon turmeric
Salt, to taste

1 Put the corn into a pot with enough water to cover it and bring to a boil. Reduce the heat and cook until tender (just a few minutes). Drain (save some water for the curry) and set aside.

2 Meanwhile, make the curry paste. Heat half the oil in a kadhai or heavy pan. Add the whole spices and fry for 1 minute. Then add the onion and stir-fry until brown.

3 Add the coconut and continue stirring until the whole mixture is a rich brown. Remove from the heat and let it cool. Add a little water and grind to a fine paste in a blender. Set aside.

4 In another pan, heat the remaining oil and add the cumin seeds. When they darken, add the corn and mix well.

5 Mix in the tomatoes, remaining spices, and salt. Add a few tablespoons of the reserved corn water.

6 Gently stir in the curry paste and simmer for 3 minutes to blend well. Add more water if necessary to make a thick sauce.

broccoli with cumin and garlic
broccoli bhaji

This stir-fry would traditionally be made with cauliflower but, with broccoli being more and more available in India, it has been adapted to this vegetable as well. Broccoli is very light and easy to digest and makes a great summer meal. It is also rich in vitamins A and C. I find that the combination of garlic and broccoli is really delicious and, for my garlic-loving friends, I leave the cloves whole instead of crushing them.

Serves: 4
Preparation time: 10 minutes
Cooking time: 20 minutes

2 tablespoons sunflower oil
$1/2$ teaspoon black mustard seeds
$1/2$ teaspoon cumin seeds
Pinch of asafetida
2 cloves garlic, minced
$1/2$ teaspoon turmeric
10 ounces broccoli, cut into florets
  (about 5–6 cups)
Salt, to taste

1 Heat the oil in a heavy pan and add the mustard seeds. When they pop, add the cumin seeds and the asafetida. When the cumin seeds darken, add the garlic and turmeric. Almost at once, add the broccoli and season with salt.

2 Pour in a couple of tablespoons of water and cook uncovered, adding a bit more water if necessary, until the florets are done but still a bit crisp. Serve hot with rotis.

spicy parsee-style stew
laganshala

Lagan means wedding and this stew is often served at Parsee weddings which are known for their delicious feasts. Parsee cooking is influenced by many world cuisines and therefore it is not unusual to find ingredients such as Worcestershire sauce in their recipes. This sweet, sour, and spicy stew goes well with Pilaf (page 77).

Serves: 4
Preparation time: 15 minutes
Cooking time: 40 minutes

3 cloves garlic
5 dried red chiles, seeded and soaked in
  water for a couple of minutes
1 teaspoon cumin seeds
Sunflower oil for frying
5 ounces mixed potatoes and sweet potatoes,
  peeled and cubed (about 1 cup)
5 ounces carrots, peeled and cubed
  (about 1¹/₃ cups)
1 large onion, sliced
Salt, to taste
8 cherry tomatoes
1 tablespoon Worcestershire sauce
1 tablespoon malt vinegar (if unavailable,
  use cider or wine vinegar)
1 teaspoon sugar

1 Whizz the garlic, red chiles, and cumin seeds into a fine paste in a coffee grinder. You could use a mortar and pestle if this is easier.

2 Heat 2 tablespoons of the oil in a deep frying pan and fry the potatoes and sweet potatoes until golden and just tender, then drain on paper towels and set aside. In the same pan, fry the carrots for a couple of minutes, turning them, then drain and set aside.

3 Heat another 2 tablespoons of oil in a heavy pan and fry the onions until golden. Add the garlic-chile-cumin paste and fry for 1 minute over low heat. Add a few tablespoons of water to prevent it from sticking and cook for 2–3 minutes.

4 Add the fried vegetables and season with salt. Pour in about ¹/₄ cup of water and blend the mixture well. Bring to a boil and add the cherry tomatoes, Worcestershire sauce, vinegar, and sugar. Cook for 5 minutes until the tomatoes soften and the sauce is thick, adding more water as necessary to make a thick stew. Serve hot.

baby gourds with garlic
tendlichi talasani

Tendli or tindora are small gourds each the size of a little finger. They are becoming available in the West both fresh and frozen. The best tindora are bright green and crisp. When they get stale, they turn crinkly and the insides go from pale green to orange. Their rather neutral taste needs strong flavoring. This recipe can also be used for potatoes instead of the tindora.

Serves: 4
Preparation time: 15 minutes
Cooking time: 25 minutes

2 tablespoons sunflower oil
¹/₂ teaspoon black mustard seeds
¹/₂ teaspoon cumin seeds
3 dried red chiles, seeded
Pinch of asafetida
3 cloves garlic, lightly crushed and left in
  the skin
10 ounces tindora, sliced lengthwise
¹/₂ teaspoon turmeric
Salt, to taste

1 Heat the oil in a heavy, shallow pan and fry the mustard seeds until they pop. Add the cumin and, almost immediately, add the chiles and asafetida.

2 Fry the garlic until it turns golden and add the tindora. Sprinkle in the turmeric and season with salt. Mix well. Pour in 2 tablespoons of water, cover the pan, and bring to a boil. Reduce the heat and simmer until the tindora is cooked but still has a crunch, for about 15 minutes. Cook over high heat, stirring frequently, to get rid of any liquid. Serve hot with rotis.

crushed yam with chile and garlic
suranacha thecha

Yam is popular in the west of India where it is known as suran. Be careful while peeling certain varieties of suran as the sap can cause a mild itching of the hands. The trick is to oil them lightly before handling all varieties of yam. On cooking, yam develops a creamy, mild potato-like taste, without being floury.

Serves: 4
Preparation time: 15 minutes
Cooking time: 30 minutes

10 ounces yam, peeled, washed, and cut into
 $1/2$-inch cubes (about 2 cups)
1 tablespoon sunflower oil
$1/2$ teaspoon black mustard seeds
Pinch of asafetida
2 fresh small green chiles, finely chopped
1 teaspoon ginger-garlic paste (page 11)
1 teaspoon turmeric
Salt, to taste
2 teaspoons crushed peanuts
Handful of cilantro leaves, chopped
Large pinch of sugar

1 Put the yam in a heavy saucepan, cover with water, and bring to a boil. Reduce the heat and simmer until it is just tender, each cube being cooked through but still holding its shape. Drain and set aside.

2 Heat the oil in another pan and fry the mustard seeds for 1 minute until they pop. Add the asafetida, green chiles, and the ginger-garlic paste. Reduce the heat and fry for a couple of minutes, stirring.

3 Stir in the turmeric and add the reserved cooked yam. Turn up the heat, season with salt, and stir to blend. Don't worry if the yam disintegrates a bit—it is meant to!

4 Add the peanuts, cilantro, and sugar, mix lightly, and remove from the heat. Serve hot with rotis (page 32) or poories (page 74).

green peas with cumin and ginger
vatana bhaaji

This is a fresh looking and great tasting stir-fry. I sometimes use it to fill wraps, adding a few sliced tomatoes and then offer it to the kids for a weekend lunch. You can sprinkle a bit of coconut on top for variety and also stir in a few spoonfuls of Greek yogurt for an instant summer salad. This goes well with poories (page 74).

Serves: 4
Preparation time: nil
Cooking time: 15 minutes

2 tablespoons sunflower oil
$1/2$ teaspoon cumin seeds
$21/2$ cups green peas
$1/2$ teaspoon turmeric
2 fresh small green chiles, slit down the
 middle but kept whole with the stalk
Pinch of sugar
Salt, to taste
$3/4$-inch piece of fresh ginger, peeled

1 Heat the oil in a kadhai or saucepan and add the cumin seeds.

2 As they sizzle, add the green peas and stir. Sprinkle in the turmeric and add the green chiles. Stir for 1 minute.

3 Pour in a couple of tablespoons of water, add the sugar and salt, and bring to a boil. Reduce the heat and cook, uncovered, until the peas are soft.

4 Remove from the heat, grate the ginger over the top, and gently fold it in with a wooden spoon. Serve warm.

puffy fried bread
poories

Poories are fried and therefore rich in taste (and calories!). They form a part of a wedding feast or banquet and are sometimes flavored or stuffed with spices and herbs. They are often served with fresh mango puree or a yogurt-based dessert called shrikhand and this is quite usual in India—in a traditional meal, the dessert is always served as a part of the main meal.

Serves: 4
Preparation time: 15 minutes
Cooking time: 20 minutes

2^1/$_3$ cups whole wheat flour, plus extra
  for flouring
Sunflower oil for deep-frying
^{2}/$_3$ cup warm water

1 Blend the flour, 1 tablespoon of oil, and enough of the warm water to make a stiff dough. You may need a little less or more water than the quantity given, depending upon the quality of flour. Divide the dough into equal balls, the size of a large cherry. Smear your palms with oil and smooth each ball.

2 Heat the oil in a deep frying pan or kadhai. Roll each ball out into a flat disc about 3/4 inch in diameter, flouring the board as necessary. Gently place the disc into the hot oil, pressing it down with the back of a slotted spoon until puffy and golden. Turn it over and fry for 1 minute. It will puff up only if the oil is hot enough and the disc has been submerged. Lift it out with a slotted spoon and drain on absorbent paper. Continue in the same way for all the poories, adjusting the heat so that the poories do not brown excessively.

fenugreek leaf bread
thepla

This is the ideal bread to take on picnics or long journeys. It keeps well because of its yogurt content and stays soft for a couple of days. It is eaten with a spicy mango chutney. Fenugreek leaves can be bought in Indian grocery stores in bundles. You need to pinch the leaves off and discard the stalks. The leaves are often dried to make kasuri methi, and used for giving many curries a distinctive curry smell.

Serves: 4
Preparation time: 20 minutes
Cooking time: 30 minutes

2^1/$_3$ cups whole wheat flour, plus extra
  for flouring
1 cup chickpea flour (besan)
2 handfuls of fenugreek leaves, washed and
  finely chopped
^{1}/$_2$ teaspoon chili powder
^{1}/$_2$ teaspoon cumin seeds
1 tablespoon sunflower oil plus extra
  for brushing
^{3}/$_4$ cup plain yogurt
Salt, to taste

1 Combine the two flours, fenugreek, chili powder, and cumin seeds in a mixing bowl and mix well with your fingers.

2 Drizzle in the oil and mix again. Pour in enough yogurt to make a firm dough and season with salt, before kneading well to bring everything together.

3 Divide the dough into portions the size of a lime. Coat them lightly with flour, shape into a ball in your palm, and flatten slightly. Roll out into flat discs, 4 inches in diameter, flouring the board as necessary.

4 Heat a griddle or shallow pan. Cook the discs until the surface appears bubbly. Turn over and press the edges down with a clean cloth to cook evenly. As soon as brown spots appear, the thepla is done. Make sure that the thepla is cooked evenly all over. You can do this by cooking them over medium heat and raising the temperature if the pan cools down.

5 Remove, brush with oil, and keep warm by enclosing in aluminum foil. Cook all the theplas in the same way.

sindhi-style rotis
koki

This is a favorite of the Sindhi community. They are fond of spicy, rich food but I have used far less oil than a traditional Sindhi cook would!

Serves: 4
Preparation time: 15 minutes
Cooking time: 40 minutes

$2^1/_3$ cups whole wheat flour, plus extra
  for flouring
1 medium onion, finely chopped
2 fresh small green chiles, finely chopped
Handful of cilantro leaves, chopped
Salt, to taste
2 tablespoons sunflower oil plus extra
  for brushing

1 Combine the flour, onion, green chiles, and cilantro in a large mixing bowl. Season with salt and add the oil to the mixture.

2 Blend all the ingredients with your fingers and add enough warm water to form a firm dough. Knead for 5 minutes or so but make sure that the dough is not too soft. Let it rest for about 5 minutes.

3 Divide the dough into 8 lime-sized balls. Flour the board and roll out each ball into a thick disc about $3^1/_4$ inches in diameter.

4 Heat a flat pan over medium heat and place a koki in it. When the underside begins to brown, brush the top with oil and turn it over to cook the oiled side. Make sure that both sides are cooked by keeping the flame at medium. Brush the first side with oil and remove. Make the rest of the kokis in the same way. Serve hot with a hot mango relish and plain yogurt.

plain boiled rice
bhaat

This is the simplest form of cooked rice and is the one most commonly eaten all over India. Its neutral, unflavored taste goes well with the spices in the accompanying curries and stir-fries. In Maharashtra and Gujarat, people use many local varieties of rice such as ambemohar or surti kolam. These are quite fragrant and delicious. However, I have used basmati rice in this recipe as it is quite easily found outside India, almost anywhere in the world. Also, I never add salt to plain rice—it simply isn't needed.

Serves: 4
Preparation time: 5 minutes
Cooking time: 20 minutes

1¹/₂ **cups basmati rice, washed and drained**
3 cups hot water

1 Put the ingredients in a heavy saucepan and bring to a boil. Reduce the heat, cover, and simmer for 10 minutes until the rice is fluffy and cooked. This may take a bit more or less time depending upon the age and quality of the rice. In the West it is difficult to find out the age of the rice but in India people will ask the grocer for old rice that cooks better without becoming sticky.

2 Gently run a fork through the rice to loosen the individual grains and serve hot with a lentil or vegetable curry.

spiced vegetable rice
pilaf

This wonderfully glamorous dish can also be made with brown rice, but takes a bit longer to cook. Brown rice has more fiber than basmati and is high in Vitamin B. I like its rough taste combined with the smoothness of the vegetables and raisins. You could jazz up this pilaf with mushrooms or mixed peppers.

Serves: 4
Preparation time: 15 minutes
Cooking time: 30 minutes

6 tablespoons sunflower oil
2 tablespoons cashews
1 tablespoon cumin seeds
5 ounces carrots, peeled and finely chopped (about 1 cup)
1¹/₄ **cups fresh or frozen green peas**
²/₃ **cup fresh or frozen corn**
Salt, to taste
1 teaspoon garam masala
1¹/₂ **cups basmati rice, washed and drained**
2 tablespoons raisins

1 Heat the oil in a heavy pan and fry the cashews until golden. Drain and set aside.

2 Add the cumin seeds to the pan. When they pop, add the vegetables and salt, then stir in the garam masala.

3 Add the rice and fry until translucent, before pouring in 3 cups of hot water; mix gently and bring to a boil. Lower the heat, cover, and simmer for about 10–15 minutes, until the vegetables are soft but still crisp.

4 Serve hot garnished with the raisins and reserved cashews.

parsee-style coconut and cashew rice
kaju saathe khichdi pulao

A khichdi is a rice dish made with either vegetables or nuts or lentils. The texture of a khichdi can vary from firm to almost risotto-like and many khichdis are almost soupy. They are considered very healthy and nutritious and often someone who is convalescing will be offered khichdi to boost their energy levels! This one is quite festive and warming on a cold evening.

Serves: 4
Preparation time: 10 minutes
Cooking time: 35 minutes

3 tablespoons sunflower oil or ghee
1 medium onion, sliced
10 black peppercorns
3 cloves
3 green cardamom pods, bruised
2 bay leaves
1 1/2 cups basmati rice, washed and drained
1 1/2 cups canned coconut milk
Salt, to taste
1 green pepper, seeded and sliced
3 tablespoons frozen green peas
2 tablespoons raisins
2 tablespoons cashews

1 Heat 2 tablespoons of the oil or ghee in a heavy saucepan and fry the onion until golden brown. Add the whole spices and bay leaves and swirl around for 1 minute. Add about 1 1/2 cups of water and bring to a boil.

2 Add the rice to the pan along with half the coconut milk and some salt. Return to a boil, then reduce the heat and add the green pepper and peas.

3 As soon as the liquid has been absorbed, add the rest of the coconut milk. Cover the pan and simmer until the rice is cooked through.

4 Heat the remaining oil or ghee in a small saucepan and fry the raisins and cashews for 1 minute. Pour them over the rice to garnish, and serve hot with Laganshala (page 70).

rice and mung bean stew
mung khichdi

Khichdis are at the heart of Pancha Karma or Ayurvedic cleansing therapy, because they are easy to digest and they promote lubrication. Various spices are added for specific functions. This khichdi is a meal in itself with good amounts of protein, carbohydrate, and fat, and combined with a vegetable stir-fry and a fresh salad, can be one of the healthiest Indian meals.

Serves: 4
Preparation time: 10 minutes
Cooking time: 35 minutes

1 tablespoon ghee (or sunflower oil if you prefer)
5 cloves
10 black peppercorns
1 bay leaf
1/2 teaspoon cumin seeds
1/2 teaspoon turmeric
1 1/3 cups basmati rice, washed and drained
1/4 cup split mung beans, washed and drained
Salt, to taste

1 Heat the ghee in a large heavy saucepan and fry the cloves, peppercorns, bay leaf, and cumin seeds for about 1 minute until the aroma fills the kitchen.

2 Add the turmeric, rice, mung beans, salt, and 3 cups of hot water and bring to a boil. Reduce the heat and simmer, covered, until the rice is creamy and soft, for about 30 minutes, adding more hot water as necessary. This dish will be quite moist which only increases its digestibility. Serve with plain yogurt on the side.

stir-fried mung bean sprouts
mugachi usal

The process of sprouting induces a riot of bio-chemical changes in which complex components break down into simpler substances that are easy to digest. Sprouted legumes have higher amounts of vitamin C, iron, and calcium than those that are not sprouted. Sprouted beans are a common addition to a Maharashtrian or Gujarati meal and are a must in a thali from this region.

Serves: 4
Preparation time: 10 minutes + 5 hours
  soaking time + overnight sprouting time
Cooking time: 25 minutes

3/4 cup dried mung beans
1 tablespoon sunflower oil
1/2 teaspoon black mustard seeds
1/2 teaspoon cumin seeds
8 curry leaves
1 small fresh small green chile, cut in half
  and seeded
1 medium onion, finely chopped
1/4 teaspoon turmeric
Salt, to taste
2 tablespoons dry, unsweetened coconut
1 tablespoon chopped cilantro leaves
1 tablespoon lemon juice

1 Soak the mung beans in cold water for 5 hours, then drain them and tie them in cheese cloth and put in a warm place to sprout overnight. Refresh the bean sprouts in cold water and set aside.

2 Heat the oil and add the mustard seeds. When they pop, add the cumin seeds, curry leaves, and the green chile. Swirl them around and add the onion, frying it until soft.

3 Tip in the bean sprouts, turmeric, and some salt. Add about 3 tablespoons of water and bring to a boil. Reduce the heat, cover the pan, and cook until the sprouts are soft but firm, for about 20 minutes, adding more water if necessary.

4 Finish off by sprinkling the coconut, cilantro, and lemon juice on top. Serve warm.

maharashtrian sweet and sour lentils
aamti

I have often been asked during my cooking demonstrations about the cooking of lentils. My advice is to wash them well and cook them in plenty of water. They should mash up in the cooking process and if you have to use a whisk or beater, it often means that they need more cooking time. This recipe uses jaggery (palm sugar) which is manufactured commercially in Maharashtra. Soft brown sugar makes an acceptable substitute.

Serves: 4
Preparation time: 10 minutes
Cooking time: 35 minutes

3/4 cup yellow lentils (toor dal)
2 tablespoons sunflower oil
1/2 teaspoon black mustard seeds
Large pinch asafetida
1/2 teaspoon cumin seeds
10 curry leaves
2 fresh small green chiles, sliced
1/2 teaspoon turmeric
2 tomatoes, chopped
1 tablespoon jaggery or soft brown sugar
Salt, to taste
Juice of 1/2 lemon
Small handful of cilantro leaves, chopped

lentil fritters
moong dal bhajia

1 Bring the lentils to a boil in 1¹/₂ cups of hot water and simmer until soft and mushy, adding more water as necessary. This should take about 30 minutes. I usually cover the pan partially when the simmering starts, to hasten the process. Set aside the cooked lentils which should have a thick, custard-like consistency.

2 Heat the oil in a saucepan and add the mustard seeds. When they pop, add the asafetida, cumin, curry leaves, and chiles, and fry for 1 minute.

3 Tip in the turmeric and add the cooked lentils at once.

4 Bring to a boil. Add the tomatoes, jaggery or sugar, and salt, and turn off the heat. The tomatoes should turn mushy in the pot. Stir in the lemon juice and top with the cilantro.

5 Serve hot with plain, boiled rice (page 77).

Every Indian meal is served with accompaniments and in the western region of Rajasthan and Gujarat these are usually fried. Pakoras (also called bhajias) are common all over India and can also be added to yogurt to make another traditional accompaniment, Dahi Vada. Pakoras can be served as cocktail snacks or after-school snacks for when the kids come home from school. They make a great alternative to fries!

Serves: 4
Preparation time: 15 minutes
Cooking time: 30 minutes

³/₄ cup split mung beans, washed and
   soaked for 1 hour
2 fresh small green chiles, minced
Small handful of cilantro leaves,
   finely chopped
¹/₂ teaspoon coriander seeds,
   coarsely crushed
¹/₂ teaspoon cumin seeds, coarsely crushed
¹/₂ teaspoon ajowan seeds (optional,
   although they taste great!)
Salt, to taste
Sunflower oil for deep-frying

1 Drain the soaked mung beans and put them into a blender with about ¹/₃ cup water. Whizz until coarsely ground. The batter should be quite thick.

3 Heat the oil in a kadhai or deep frying pan. When it is quite hot, spoon out 3 tablespoons of the oil and add it to the lentil batter. Mix well, as this will make the pakoras crisp.

4 Using a tablespoon, drop spoonfuls of the lentil batter into the hot oil, 2–3 at a time depending upon the size of the pan. Lower the heat to medium and fry the pakoras until golden brown.

5 Make sure that they are cooked through and then continue in the same way with the rest of the batter.

6 Serve hot with ketchup and papaya chutney (page 89).

gujarati-style spinach with lentils
palak dal

Many regions in India combine lentils with vegetables to add flavor, nutrition, and variety to a meal. I sometimes use fresh fenugreek leaves or even greens in this recipe. I like the vegetables to be really finely chopped so that they almost melt into the lentils. That is why I have suggested that you whizz the spinach in a blender.

Serves: 4
Preparation time: 10 minutes
Cooking time: 40 minutes

3/4 cup split mung beans, washed
 and drained
5 ounces fresh spinach
 (about 3 large handfuls), washed,
 drained, and chopped
2 tablespoons sunflower oil or ghee
1/2 teaspoon black mustard seeds
1/2 teaspoon cumin seeds
1 teaspoon peeled and grated fresh ginger
1/2 teaspoon garlic, minced
2 fresh small green chiles, finely chopped
Juice of 1/2 lemon
Salt, to taste

1 Put the lentils in a heavy saucepan and add 1¹/2 cups of hot water. Bring to a boil, reduce the heat, and simmer, covered, until the lentils are mushy, for about 25 minutes.

2 In the meantime, put the spinach in a blender and pulse 4–5 times, until it is quite fine but not mushy. Add the spinach to the lentils and let them cook for 3–4 minutes.

3 Heat the oil or ghee in a small saucepan and add the mustard seeds. When they pop, add the cumin, then the ginger, garlic, and green chiles almost at once. Pour this into the cooked lentils and simmer for 1 minute more. Remove from the heat.

4 Squeeze in the lemon juice and season with salt. Serve hot with plain rice and a good vegetable stir-fry.

curried black chickpeas
kala channa masala

This has to be one of the simplest recipes ever. You can substitute the black chickpeas with white ones. Black ones are coarser in taste and often associated with feasts cooked in honor of the Mother Goddess. Asafetida is always added to beans and lentils to make them more digestible and to lessen flatulence.

Serves: 4
Preparation time: 10 minutes
Cooking time: 10 minutes

1/2 teaspoon turmeric
1 teaspoon ground cumin
1 teaspoon ground coriander
1/2 teaspoon chili powder
2 tablespoons sunflower oil
Pinch of asafetida
Salt, to taste
15-ounce can black chickpeas, drained
1 tablespoon lemon juice
Few cilantro leaves, chopped

1 Mix all the spice powders with about 1/4 cup of water and set aside.

2 Heat the oil in a heavy saucepan and add the asafetida. Reduce the heat, stand back, and pour in the spice liquid. Let it sizzle for 1 minute or so and add the salt and the chickpeas.

3 Pour in about 2/3 cup of hot water and bring to a boil. Simmer for a couple of minutes, crushing a few of the chickpeas with the back of the spoon to thicken the sauce. This should be fairly liquid but still have some consistency. Remove from the heat and serve hot, sprinkled with the lemon juice and cilantro.

tangy lentils with crisp bread
dal pakwan

This is a popular Sindhi breakfast but I could eat it at any time of the day. The lentils must be cooked until soft but should still hold their shape. I soak them for at least 5–6 hours but, if you forget to do that (and I sometimes do), be prepared for a slightly longer cooking time. Also, this dish tastes so much more delicious when made with ghee rather than with oil. Serve with some sliced onions and a wedge of lemon and enjoy with friends!

Serves: 4
Preparation time: 15 minutes + soaking time
Cooking time: 1 hour

For the dal:
3/4 cup channa dal (split chickpea lentils), washed and soaked for 5–6 hours
1/4 teaspoon turmeric
1 tablespoon tamarind concentrate
Salt, to taste
1 tablespoon ghee
1/2 teaspoon garam masala
1/2 teaspoon red chili powder
1/2 teaspoon ground cumin
1/2 teaspoon amchoor (dried mango) powder

For the pakwan:
2 1/3 cups all-purpose flour, plus extra for flouring
1 tablespoon ghee
Pinch of salt
Sunflower oil for deep-frying

To make the dal:

1 Put the lentils in a heavy saucepan with 1 1/2 cups of water and bring to a boil. Add the turmeric and, when boiling, reduce the heat and simmer until the lentils are cooked, for about 30 minutes. The dal should not be mushy. I like to see the shape of the lentils rather than a sludge!

2 Stir in the tamarind concentrate and season with salt.

3 Heat the ghee in a small pan. When nearly smoking hot, remove from the heat and add all the remaining spices. Pour this over the cooked dal at once or else the spices will burn. Serve hot with the crisp bread or pakwan.

To make the pakwan:

1 Mix the flour, ghee, and salt, and add enough warm water to make a soft dough.

2 Knead well, then divide the dough into cherry-sized balls and roll out into thin discs 3 1/4 inches in diameter. Flour the board as necessary to prevent sticking.

3 Prick the discs all over with a fork.

4 Heat the oil in a deep pan or kadhai. When nearly smoking, reduce the heat and gently slide the pakwans in one at a time. Fry them until golden and crisp.

5 Drain and keep them warm in aluminum foil while you make the rest of the pakwans in the same way.

silky pumpkin in yogurt
bhoplyache bharit

I love this dish for the sweet and silky feel that the pumpkin takes on when added to the yogurt. Peel as thinly as possible, and be sure to get rid of the seeds and membranes. I chop the chile very finely or even bash it in a mortar as I think that there are few things worse than biting into a piece of chile unintentionally!

Serves: 4
Preparation time: 15 minutes
Cooking time: 10 minutes

**10 ounces red pumpkin, peeled and cubed
(about 2 cups)**
$1/4$ cup plain yogurt
Few cilantro leaves, chopped
1 fresh small green chile, finely chopped
Salt, to taste
$3/4$ teaspoon sugar
2 teaspoons sunflower oil
1 teaspoon black mustard seeds
$1/2$ teaspoon asafetida

1 Put the pumpkin in a pan with enough hot water to cover it and bring to a boil. Reduce the heat and simmer for 3–4 minutes until soft. Drain the pumpkin (reserving the liquid if you like) and mash the pumpkin with a fork. (You can use the cooking liquid in a lentil dish or even for boiling rice.)

2 Add the yogurt, cilantro, chile, salt, and sugar to the pumpkin and transfer to a dish.

3 Heat the oil in a small pan and add the mustard seeds. As they start popping, add the asafetida. Pour this over the pumpkin at once. Serve cool.

gujarati-style yogurt curry
gujarati kadhi

The real flavor of this curry is in the tempering, where spice seeds are fried in hot oil and then poured over it. I love the fenugreek seeds that smell rather sweet but have a bitter taste. This dish can be tricky sometimes as the yogurt can split on cooking; to avoid this, use low heat and stir frequently. Kadhi is served with Mung Khichdi (page 79) and hot pickle.

Serves: 4
Preparation time: 15 minutes
Cooking time: 25 minutes

1¹/3 cups plain yogurt
6 tablespoons chickpea flour
3 cups water
Salt, to taste
1 tablespoon sugar
1 tablespoon sunflower oil
¹/2 teaspoon black mustard seeds
¹/2 teaspoon cumin seeds
Few curry leaves
¹/4 teaspoon fenugreek seeds
10 black peppercorns
6 cloves
4 dried red chiles, seeded and broken up

1 Whisk the yogurt, flour, water, salt, and sugar to a smooth mixture. Pour it into a heavy saucepan and cook over high heat for 3–4 minutes. Reduce the heat and continue cooking, stirring frequently, until the curry is creamy. This should take about 15 minutes. The test is in the aroma that should not be of raw flour. Remove from the heat and pour into a warmed dish.

2 Heat the oil in a small pan and add the mustard seeds. When they crackle, add all the remaining ingredients. Swirl the pan for 1 minute and pour the oil and the spices over the yogurt curry.

3 Serve hot. Gujarati kadhi can be made ahead of time, in which case reheat gently, taking care not to let the curry boil.

chickpea flour dumplings in spices
gatte kisubzi

A typical Rajasthani dish, this has quite a bit of oil and chili powder and makes an occasional, indulgent treat, not for the faint hearted, with a roti or poories. The yogurt must not be overheated as it will curdle.

Serves: 4
Preparation time: 10 minutes
Cooking time: 25 minutes

1 cup chickpea flour (besan)
1 teaspoon ground coriander
1¹/2 teaspoons red chili powder
1 teaspoon turmeric
Salt, to taste
4 tablespoons ghee or sunflower oil
³/4 cup plain yogurt
¹/2 teaspoon cumin seeds

1 Mix the flour with ¹/2 teaspoon each of the coriander, the chili powder, and the turmeric. Season with salt. Pour in 2 tablespoons of the ghee or oil, and enough water to make a stiff dough. Knead well. Make 4 thin, long rolls of the dough. Boil a pan of water and put the rolls in to simmer for 5–7 minutes. Drain and let cool slightly. Cut these rolls into small pieces called gatte.

2 In a heavy saucepan, combine the yogurt with another ¹/2 teaspoon each of the coriander, chili, and turmeric. Add the gatte and heat well without letting them boil. Simmer for 5 minutes and remove from the heat.

3 Warm the remaining ghee or oil in a small saucepan. Add the cumin seeds and, as they turn dark, add the remaining chili powder. Pour this into the yogurt mixture and serve hot.

carrot and dried fruit relish
gajar meva nu achaar

Whenever my Parsee friends invite me to a traditional wedding feast, I make sure to eat a good portion of lagan nu achaar which is the special wedding relish with many kinds of dried fruit and berries. This is a simpler version of that sweet and sour relish and one that goes well with hot dal and rice.

Serves: 4
Preparation time: 15 minutes + overnight soaking
Cooking time: 40 minutes

2 tablespoons raisins
8 dried apricots, thinly sliced
6 dates, thinly sliced
2/3 cup malt vinegar
5 ounces carrots, peeled and grated (about 1 cup)
3/4 cup sugar
1/2 teaspoon garlic powder
1/2 teaspoon garam masala
1/2 teaspoon turmeric
1/2 teaspoon chili powder
Salt, to taste

1 Soak the dried fruit overnight in 3 tablespoons of the vinegar.

2 To make the relish, place the carrots, sugar, and the remaining vinegar in a heavy saucepan and cook over high heat until the sugar begins to melt, but take care not to let it burn.

3 Add the garlic powder, reduce the heat, and continue cooking until the carrots are soft.

4 Add the soaked, dried fruit and cook for about 5 minutes to blend.

5 Sprinkle in the remaining spices and season with salt. Cook until thick and syrupy. Remove from the heat, cool thoroughly, and store in a clean, dry glass jar. This will keep for a couple of months in the fridge.

papaya chutney with mustard seeds
papaya chutney

There are countless papaya farms in Maharashtra, therefore the fruit is inexpensive and sold very fresh. Indian papayas can be large, and vary between the size of a honeydew melon and a watermelon! In fact, the little papayas we see in the West are known as disco papaya and are a novelty. Preparing a papaya means removing all the seeds and pith around the center and, because it is so soft when ripe, this fruit hardly needs any cooking at all.

Serves: 4
Preparation time: 10 minutes
Cooking time: 10 minutes

1/3 cup malt vinegar
1/3 cup sugar
1/4 cup water
5 ounces ripe papaya, peeled, seeds discarded, and flesh cubed (about 1 cup)
1/2 teaspoon garam masala
Salt, to taste
1 teaspoon sunflower oil
1 teaspoon black mustard seeds

1 To make the chutney, put the vinegar, sugar, and water in a heavy saucepan and bring to a boil. Reduce the heat and simmer until syrupy. Add in the papaya and garam masala, and cook for a few minutes, stirring constantly. Season with salt and remove from the heat. Set aside.

2 Heat the oil in a small saucepan and add the mustard seeds. When they pop, pour them over the chutney and mix well. Serve with rice and Kadhi (page 81). This chutney will keep for 1–2 days in the fridge.

potato and garlic balls encased in batter
batata vada

A classic dish from Maharashtra and one that is sold on every street corner in Mumbai. It is often eaten as a mid-morning snack or served in the afternoon with a cup of sweet tea. I prefer to use baking potatoes for this to get a really buttery texture but you can choose any variety you like. Eat these fresh, as keeping them for any length of time makes the outer shell of batter go limp.

Serves: 4
Preparation time: 30 minutes
Cooking time: 15 minutes

10 ounces potatoes, peeled, boiled, and
   mashed (about 1^1/$_3$ cups)
Salt, to taste
^{1}/$_2$ teaspoon turmeric
2 tablespoons chopped cilantro leaves
2 fresh small green chiles, finely chopped
2 cloves garlic, finely chopped
2 tablespoons sunflower oil
1 teaspoon black mustard seeds
Large pinch of asafetida
1 teaspoon cumin seeds

For the batter:
1 cup chickpea flour (besan)
Large pinch of baking soda
^{1}/$_2$ teaspoon turmeric
Salt, to taste
Sunflower oil for deep-frying

1 Combine the potatoes, salt, turmeric, cilantro, green chiles, and garlic in a mixing bowl.

2 Heat the oil in a small pan and add the mustard seeds. When they crackle, add the asafetida and cumin seeds. Pour this into the potato mixture and mix well.

3 Divide the potato mixture into 8 small balls and set aside.

4 Make a batter of pouring consistency with the flour, baking soda, turmeric, and salt, and as much water as is needed.

5 Heat the oil in a deep frying pan or kadhai.

6 When it is nearly smoking, dip each potato ball in the batter and deep-fry it until golden. Reduce the heat to prevent the balls from browning too quickly. Serve hot with ketchup as a snack or with a main meal as an accompaniment.

bananas stuffed with cilantro chutney
bharela kela

If you have ever wondered what to do with slightly overripe bananas that have not gone mushy, here is the perfect recipe. Traditionally these are made with ripe plantains which are firm and sweet, but dessert bananas also work well too. My mother makes these for me even now as a special treat and, unusual as they may sound, they taste delicious with everything. I like them a little over-fried with a few burnt bits.

Serves: 4
Preparation time: 15 minutes
Cooking time: 15 minutes

2 good handfuls of cilantro leaves
3 cloves garlic, peeled
1^1/$_4$-inch piece of ginger, peeled and chopped
2 fresh small green chiles, roughly chopped
^{1}/$_4$ cup dry, unsweetened coconut
Salt, to taste
^{1}/$_2$ teaspoon sugar
4 ripe but firm bananas
Sunflower oil for shallow frying

1 Put the cilantro into a blender along with the garlic, ginger, chiles, and coconut.

2 Whizz to a fine paste with a few tablespoons of water. Season with salt and add the sugar. Mix well and set aside.

3 Peel the bananas and make a shallow slit along the top of each one, keeping them whole. Stuff a little of the coriander chutney into each banana. Any extra chutney can be served on the side or frozen for later use. (The chutney makes an excellent accompaniment to a meal and freezes very well.)

4 Heat some oil in a wide pan and shallow-fry the bananas, turning them occasionally until they are golden brown and slightly caramelized. Serve warm.

black-eyed peas with coconut and raisins
lobhia ka salad

This is a great all-rounder, good for lunch, brunch, or to accompany a more substantial meal. Also, what could be simpler? I love the creaminess of black-eyed peas, and what a great way to add protein and fiber to a meal! I sometimes stir some plain yogurt into this salad to turn it into an exceptionally delicious raita. Toss a few finely chopped green chiles on top if you like a bit of heat.

Serves: 4
Preparation time: 10 minutes
Cooking time: nil

14-ounce can black-eyed peas, drained
Salt, to taste
$^1/_2$ teaspoon sugar
$^1/_4$ cup freshly grated or dried coconut
2 teaspoons raisins
1 teaspoon lemon juice
Few chopped cilantro leaves

Mix all the ingredients together and serve at once.

quick no-fuss mango ice cream
keri nu ice cream

Both Gujarat and Maharashtra are famous for their delicious seasonal mangoes. Kesar from the former, and Alphonso from the latter being the most popular. During the mango season in the summer, most households make all sorts of wonderful recipes from this fruit. Ice cream is very quick to make but be sure you use soft, non-fibrous mangoes. You might want to move the ice cream from the freezer to the fridge half an hour before serving it to soften it slightly.

Serves: 4
Preparation time: 30 minutes + 7–8 hours
  freezing time
Cooking time: nil

1¼ cups heavy cream
1 cup cold milk
1 cup condensed milk
1¼ cups fresh mango pulp (or canned pulp if
  using out of season)

1 Pour the cream into a mixing bowl and whip it until it is thick and fluffy, for about 3–4 minutes. Take care not to overdo this or else you will end up with butter!

2 In a separate bowl, beat the milk and condensed milk together until well blended.

3 Fold the condensed milk mixture into the whipped cream, then fold in the mango pulp as well. Tip into an ice cream tray and freeze for about 7–8 hours until firm.

mango and yogurt medley
amrakhand

This is the traditional method of making Amrakhand which tastes rich and delicious. I have a lighter version made with Greek yogurt that cuts out the hanging up of the set yogurt. Amrakhand is very popular in Maharashtra and its close cousin Shrikhand, made in exactly the same way but without the mango, is popular in Gujarat as well.

Serves: 4
Preparation time: 15 minutes + 5 hours
  draining time
Cooking time: nil

2 pints whole-milk yogurt
About 6 tablespoons sugar, or to taste
²/₃ cup mango pulp (canned or fresh)
Pinch of ground cardamom
2 tablespoons crushed pistachios

1 Tie the yogurt in a clean piece of cheesecloth and hang it up to drain off the whey. I usually do this over the kitchen sink.

2 When the yogurt is quite dry, scoop it out of the cloth and place it in a bowl. Beat well with a wooden spoon or whisk, adding the sugar a little at a time.

3 When the yogurt is light and fluffy in texture, stir in the mango pulp and cardamom, and spoon it into decorative glasses and chill. Serve sprinkled with the pistachios.

sweet sparkly diamonds
bombay ice halwa

This is a popular dessert in Mumbai (formerly known as Bombay) as is its cousin, the sticky Bombay chewy halwa. The chewy halwa is made with wheat flour and, to eat some versions of it, one needs fangs instead of teeth. This one is fine and glassy and quite delicate in taste. It keeps well in the fridge for up to a week.

Serves: 4
Preparation time: 10 minutes
Cooking time: 45 minutes

1 cup very fine semolina
$^2/_3$ cup ghee
2$^1/_2$ cups milk
1$^1/_2$ cups sugar
1 tablespoon rose water
1 tablespoon slivered almonds
$^1/_2$ teaspoon ground cardamom
Large pinch of saffron

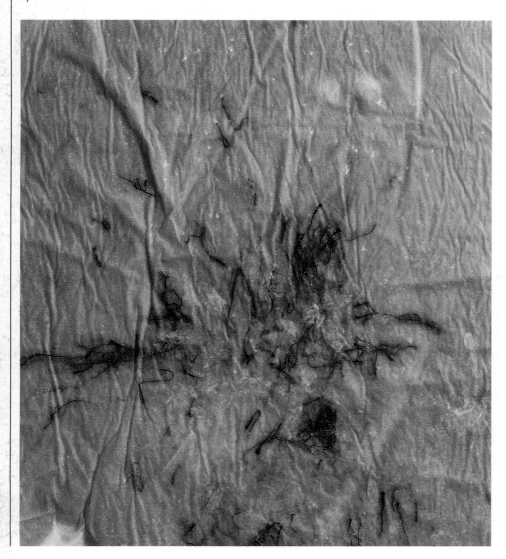

1 Put the semolina, ghee, milk, and sugar in a large, heavy saucepan and cook over high heat until the mixture begins to bubble. Reduce the heat and continue cooking, stirring all the while, until the mixture thickens into a very soft ball. Remove from the heat.

2 Add the rose water and mix well with a wooden spoon. The mixing should be almost like kneading because this brings a shine to the finished product.

3 Take a sheet of waxed paper and place a large spoonful of the semolina dough on it. Cover with another sheet and roll out the dough as quickly as possible into a thick, flat cake.

4 Remove the top sheet of paper and sprinkle some of the almonds, cardamom, and saffron strands onto the semolina cake. Replace the waxed paper on top of the cake and roll again very quickly until the dough is very thin, almost like a sheet of ice. Set it aside while you repeat with the rest of the dough.

5 Cut each sheet into roughly 16 diamond shapes and let them cool. Serve cold. Store between sheets of waxed paper to prevent the diamonds from sticking.

sweet saffron rice
keshar bhaat

This is quite a festive dish from Maharashtra although versions of it are made all over the country. I like to cook the rice until slightly soft and serve it warm, especially in the winter. The amount of ghee may seem excessive but this is quite an indulgent dessert and can be a great treat on a cold winter's evening!

Serves: 4
Preparation time: 10 minutes
Cooking time: 30 minutes

3/4 cup basmati rice, washed and drained
1/4 cup ghee
a heaping 1/3 cup sugar
Large pinch of saffron strands, soaked in
  1 tablespoon milk
1/3 cup raisins
a heaping 1/3 cup cashews, roughly crushed
Large pinch of ground cardamom

1 Put the rice in a heavy saucepan with 1 1/2 cups of hot water and bring to a boil. Reduce the heat, stir the rice, cover the pan, and simmer until cooked, for about 10 minutes.

2 Add the ghee and sugar and continue cooking over low heat, stirring constantly.

3 Add the saffron along with the milk, raisins, and cashews. Stir gently until well blended and the rice has turned a yellowy-orange color. Remove from the heat, stir in the cardamom, and serve warm.

coconut and poppy seed pastry
karanji

A favorite childhood memory of mine was eating these during Diwali, the Hindu festival of lights. My grandmother would make batches days before the festival with a strict warning that we were not to touch them until the day arrived. The temptation almost always proved too great and my cousin and I would sneak a few to eat under the table, my favorite hiding place at the time!

Serves: 4
Preparation time: 40 minutes
Cooking time: 30 minutes

2^1/$_3$ cups all-purpose flour, plus extra
  for flouring
2 teaspoons sunflower oil
Large pinch of salt

For the filling:
^{3}/$_4$ cup soft brown sugar
10 ounces freshly grated coconut
  (about 1^1/$_3$ cups) or 1^1/$_3$ cups dried
2 teaspoons white poppy seeds, dry-roasted
2 teaspoons raisins
^{1}/$_2$ teaspoon ground cardamom
Sunflower oil for deep-frying

1 Make a stiff dough with the flour, oil, salt, and water as needed. Set aside.

2 Combine the sugar, coconut, poppy seeds, raisins, and cardamom in a heavy saucepan and set over high heat. As the sugar melts, reduce the heat and cook for a few minutes to blend everything, taking care not to let the mixture burn. Remove from the heat and let the mixture cool.

3 Divide the dough into 12 equal-sized balls. Roll each one out to a thin disc about 2 inches in diameter, dusting it with a little flour if necessary.

4 Place a little of the coconut mixture in the center of the disc. If the mixture is slightly runny, strain it and use the liquid as a dipping sauce. Fold the disc in half to make a half-moon shape and seal the edges properly or the filling will come out during the frying.

5 Heat the oil in a deep frying pan and fry each pastry individually until golden. Remove with a slotted spoon and drain on absorbent paper. Serve at room temperature.

spiced tea
masala chai

If you travel through Gujarat, you will find that you are offered this version of tea everywhere. People here love sweet, spicy tea that leaves a zing on the tongue. It is especially great as an after-dinner digestive and helps to wash down the grease and spice of a meal. Fennel is known to promote good digestion and it is often boiled in water, strained out, and the water fed to even very tiny babies.

Serves: 4
Preparation time: 5 minutes
Cooking time: 15 minutes

1 teaspoon fennel seeds
5 black peppercorns
3 green cardamom pods, bruised
2^1/$_2$ cups hot water
3 teabags
Sugar, to taste
Dash of milk

1 Crush the fennel seeds, peppercorns, and cardamoms in a mortar. Put the spices in a heavy pan and pour in the water. Bring to a boil.

2 Reduce the heat and simmer for 3–4 minutes. The water will have turned golden.

3 Add the teabags and simmer for 1 minute or so. Remove from the heat, strain through a fine mesh strainer, and discard the spices and teabags.

4 Serve sweetened with sugar if you like, and add a dash of milk.

rose-flavored ice cream float
bombay falooda

Small shops that are run by the Iranians or Muslims who settled in Bombay many years ago sell this delicacy. It also has tiny subja seeds that are cooked and put at the bottom of each glass but I have omitted them in this recipe as they are so hard to find outside of India. Rose syrup is sweet, red, and fragrant and, in India, it is also mixed with water and served as rose sherbet.

Serves: 4
Preparation time: 15 minutes
Cooking time: nil

6 tablespoons rice noodles, broken into short lengths
2¹/₂ cups milk
Sugar, to taste
4 teaspoons rose syrup (available in Indian shops)
4 scoops of vanilla ice cream

1 Put the noodles in a pan with enough water to cover them and bring to a boil. Stir, reduce the heat, and simmer until soft. Drain and rinse under cold running water so that they do not get sticky.

2 In a measuring cup, mix the milk, sugar to taste, and rose syrup.

3 Divide the noodles between 4 tall glasses and pour the rose milk over them. Chill well. Just before serving, float a scoop of vanilla ice cream on top of each glass.

cumin seed cooler
jaljeera

This is a popular drink in Rajasthan and Gujarat where the summers are dry and fierce. The cumin acts as a digestive and this drink is served with main meals. Indian rock salt is mined from stone quarries and has a strong aroma that goes well with tamarind or yogurt dishes. If you cannot find rock salt, sea salt or Kosher salt can be used instead.

Serves: 4
Preparation time: 45 minutes
Cooking time: nil

2 teaspoons cumin seeds
1 tablespoon tamarind concentrate
2¹/₂ cups hot water
6 tablespoons soft brown sugar
¹/₂ teaspoon chili powder
1 teaspoon Indian rock salt (alternatively, use sea salt or Kosher salt)
Few cilantro leaves, finely chopped
Few mint leaves, finely chopped

1 Dry-roast the cumin seeds in a small pan. When they turn dark, pour into a mortar and bash them until fine and powdery. Set aside.

2 Dilute the tamarind in the water. Stir in the sugar, chili powder, salt, and reserved cumin powder, and mix well. Let the mixture cool.

3 Stir in the cilantro and mint leaves and chill the jaljeera in the fridge. Serve cold.

god masala

God Masala, which literally means sweet spice is used in certain parts of Maharashtra, such as the city of Pune, to enhance the flavor of vegetarian cooking. The masala is a black aromatic powder with a burnt sweetness which comes from the coconut in the mixture. It can be added before or after the main ingredient to vary the taste from strong to subtle. Make enough for one-time use. It can be sprinkled onto the Aamti (page 80) or the Farasbeechi Bhaji (page 67) or into a variety of lentil or vegetable dishes.

1 teaspoon sunflower oil
Seeds from 2 green cardamom pods
Small stick of cinnamon
2 cloves
1 bay leaf
5 black peppercorns
$1/2$ teaspoon coriander seeds
2 tablespoons dry, unsweetened coconut
1 teaspoon white poppy seeds

1 Heat the oil in a small saucepan and fry the cardamom seeds, cinnamon, cloves, bay leaf, peppercorns, and coriander seeds for a couple of minutes until the cloves swell.

2 Add the coconut and poppy seeds and continue cooking, stirring constantly, until the coconut is well browned.

3 Remove from the heat, cool slightly, and grind to a fine powder in a coffee grinder (or a mortar and pestle). Store in an airtight container.

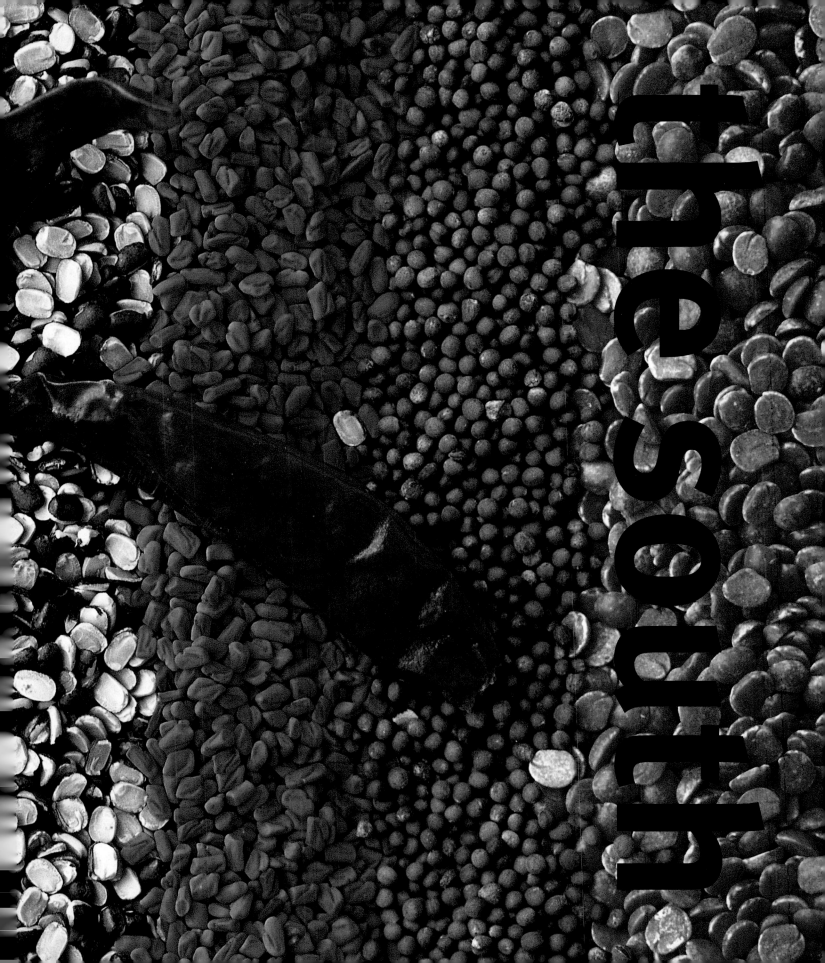

thesouth

tamil nadu

andhra pradesh

This section deals with the cooking of Tamil Nadu, Andhra Pradesh, Karnataka, Kerala, and Goa. The south was less affected by invasions (although many foreign powers did make forays) than the north and many south Indians feel that their style of cooking is the original style of India.

Tamil Nadu is situated on the southeastern coast of India by the Bay of Bengal. Some of the oldest and most famous of all Hindu temples are here, such as the Nataraja temple in Chidambaram and the Brihadeeshwara temple at Tanjore. Tamil culture is resplendent with classical literature and dance, fascinating bronze sculptures, and awe inspiring architecture. One sees the best of the Dravidian way of life here. Chennai is the capital and home to some of the finest artists and artisans in the country. Fine, shimmering silks come from Kanjeevaram, beautiful stone-studded temple jewelry is crafted in the jewelry quarter of each town. The people of Tamil Nadu are disciplined and adhere greatly to tradition. Worship, education, the arts, and food are all treated with great respect and the social order is maintained through a strict hierarchy and the passing down of knowledge about how things should be from one generation to the next. For religious reasons, most Tamilian food is vegetarian, and very fresh and fragrant. A meal here is made mainly of rice served in three different courses. First with sambhar, a thick lentil dish flavored with fresh vegetables. Then comes rasam, a thinner version of the sambhar and one that is slurped up along with the rice (a great experience!), and, finally, yogurt and rice to cool one in the strong southern heat. Other rice preparations include coconut rice, tamarind rice, lemon rice, and countless other flavorings that provide variety and taste. Black pepper, red chiles, cumin, turmeric, coriander, fenugreek, and mustard seeds are used in the cooking of vegetables such as plantains, yams, gourds, and greens.

Situated in the central south, Andhra Pradesh is a combination of Hindu vegetarianism and Muslim meat cooking. Before Partition, the beautiful city of Hyderabad was ruled by the Nizam, a man reputed to be the wealthiest in the world at the time. His kitchens produced some of the richest and tastiest fare and many of his favorite recipes have become trademarks of the region. Hyderabadi cooking is characterized by slow cooking methods. Many dishes are tempered, that is the spices are fried in hot oil and poured over the food at the last minute.

An Andhra meal is also served in courses. In Hyderabad, it is the Mughlai set of courses, replete with kabobs and biryanis. In other parts of the state, the food is mainly vegetarian and again with rice forming a staple part of it.

Andhra Pradesh is most famous for its many relishes and chutneys. The hot, spicy food is set off by chutneys made of just about anything—from mangoes, eggplants, and tomatoes to ginger and gongura, an aromatic reddish-green leafy vegetable not seen in any other state. The food of Andhra Pradesh is known for its chile heat but the combination of flavors is unique and almost addictive!

karnataka

kerala

goa

Karnataka lies just under Maharashtra and boasts of cities such as Bangalore. The Kannadigas, as the people of this state are called, are artistic and talented. Their arts and crafts, sandalwood sculptures and jewel-like silks are famous all over the country. Karnataka has also given India a classic restaurant style. Udipi, a small temple town famous for its Brahmin cooks, has a beautiful, ancient Krishna temple and the Brahmins will first offer all cooked food to the gods before serving it to devotees. The best pancakes (dosas), rice cakes (idlis), and luscious chutneys are made in Udipi, and tiny cafés that serve such food (called Udipi restaurants) can be seen in every city of India and abroad as well. They are wholly vegetarian and the food is "pure" and fragrant. Coconuts, tamarind, beans, and kokum, which is a sour purple fruit, are used in the cooking. Coconut is considered the fruit of the gods and is used in ritual worship. Every home will have a store of fresh coconuts.

My ancestors, who are Saraswat Brahmins, come from Karnataka and as a child I would spend my summers in a little village called Gokarn just off the coast. There I ate fresh curries flavored with coriander and cumin, roomfuls of mangoes, and many unusual dishes made with jackfruit and breadfruit. We would wait for the breadfruit to fall off the trees and then my aunt would peel and slice them, rub them with chile and salt, and deep-fry the slices. Heaven! Pure jaggery (palm sugar) or a slice of star fruit (carambola) was often the dessert after dinner and some of my best childhood memories are of stoning tamarind trees to get at the sour-sweet fruit.

Kerala is the southernmost state and again, it is rich in the arts. The classical dance form of Kathakali comes from here as does a variety of sculpture and craftwork. Kerala is known for its education system and for its matriarchal society where property is handed down from mother to daughter. In this state lies the Periyar wildlife reserve, home to the Indian elephant. The serving of a meal is an art form; traditionally, a banana leaf is used as a plate and all the courses are served at once. Rice, lentils, vegetables, chutneys, crisp accompaniments, and sweets, all flavored with coconut, form a fragrant feast. Curry leaves and mustard seeds are used to temper many dishes. Preparations such as thorans (vegetable stir-fries), sambhar (lentils with tamarind), and dishes cooked with plantains, yams, and cabbage are popular.

Kerala has many communities and therefore there is a great mix of cuisines. The Syrian Christians, Malabar Muslims, Jews from Cochin, and the Hindus all live and work peacefully and share a culture that is vibrant and yet gentle.

Goan food is a marvelous blend of the various influences that have been a part of the region's history. The main communities are the Christians and the Hindus. For both, the main food is fish, which is natural because Goa is on the coast and has many beautiful beaches. Fishing boats go out early into the Arabian Sea and are back, laden with seafood by dawn.

Goa was a Portuguese colony for many years and its food shows many a Portuguese influence in the Christian cooking. The Hindu fare has more or less been unaffected by them. Goan Christians eat much more meat and their specialties include vindaloos, xacuttis, and sorpotels. The exchange of recipes seems mutual. Today, Portuguese cooking boasts of arroz doce, a sweet rice preparation that is not unlike the Goan kheer or pais.

Hindu cooking is mainly from the Saraswat community that uses local produce such as coconuts, cashews, and mangoes. Spices such as asafetida, mustard seeds, and tirphal are used for flavoring many vegetables like bitter gourds, pumpkins, and plantain. Desserts are made of lentils and rice while fruits of the region include pineapples. The special liquor of Goa is feni, made with toddy or palm liquor. It is known for its fiery strength and people say that if you have been drinking it you feel its power only when you stand up!

pumpkin with cashews
tiyya gummadi

Andhra Pradesh has a long coastline along the Bay of Bengal. The cuisine is a rich variety of vegetables cooked in spices and milk. The curry leaves in this recipe add a burst of fresh flavor and, in India, they are often grown at home in pots or in the garden. They are cheap and often a vegetable seller will toss a few stalks into your bag free of charge. They are best used fresh although they can be dried for ease of storage.

Serves: 4
Preparation time: 15 minutes
Cooking time: 30 minutes

5 ounces freshly grated coconut (about 1³/4 cups) or dried
8 cashews
1 tablespoon poppy seeds
2 tablespoons sunflower oil
¹/2 teaspoon black mustard seeds
2 dried red chiles, broken in half and seeds shaken out
6 curry leaves
¹/2 teaspoon turmeric
11 ounces pumpkin, peeled and chopped into ¹/2-inch cubes (about 1¹/2–2cups)
3 tablespoons soft brown sugar
Salt, to taste
²/3 cup milk

1 Put the coconut, cashews, poppy seeds, and ¹/4 cup of water in a blender and grind to a paste. Add water as necessary to make a fine paste. Set aside.

2 Heat the oil in a heavy pan and add the mustard seeds. When they pop, add the chiles and the curry leaves. Sprinkle in the turmeric and pour in the coconut paste at once. Stir to blend.

3 Add the pumpkin and a couple of tablespoons of water.

4 Add the sugar and salt. Pour in the milk and bring to a boil. Reduce the heat and simmer until the pumpkin is just tender but still holds its shape, about 10–12 minutes. Serve hot with rice.

vegetables in yogurt
avial

This recipe is from palm-fringed Kerala where, as part of a sit-down feast, it is served on a fresh green banana leaf that is thrown away after use. Best of biodegradable! The root vegetables taste wonderful in this recipe and you can also add green peas or any kind of green beans.

Serves: 4
Preparation time: 25 minutes
Cooking time: 35 minutes

1 cup dried shredded coconut
2 fresh green chiles
¹/4 teaspoon cumin seeds
10 black peppercorns
11 ounces mixed vegetables, peeled, cubed, and steamed—potatoes, raw banana, pumpkin, yam (about 2–2¹/2 cups)
²/3 cup plain yogurt, seasoned with salt
10 curry leaves
Salt, to taste

1 Grind the coconut, chiles, cumin seeds, and peppercorns along with some water to a fine paste in a blender.

2 Add this paste to the cooked vegetables and pour in about ²/3 cup of water. Bring to a boil, then simmer for 5 minutes to blend.

3 Beat the yogurt and the salt and pour it into the pan. Simmer for a couple of minutes, then add the curry leaves and stir. Remove from the heat and serve hot with plain rice.

potatoes with green and black peppercorns
kurumulaku alu

I went to the Periyar elephant reserve in Kerala as a child and I still remember being driven through cool hills where pepper vines curl around trees and scent the air. There are more than 24 varieties of pepper grown in south India. Green peppercorns are fresher tasting than the black ones but not as hot. Some Indian stores around the world sell them fresh but they are easier to find bottled in brine.

Serves: 4
Preparation time: 10 minutes
Cooking time: 35 minutes

2 tablespoons sunflower oil
$^1/_2$ teaspoon cumin seeds
10 black peppercorns, crushed
1 large onion, finely sliced
1 teaspoon ginger-garlic paste (page 11)
4 dried red chiles
$^1/_2$ teaspoon turmeric
11 ounces potatoes, peeled and chopped into
 1-inch cubes (about 2–2$^1/_2$ cups)
Salt, to taste
3 tablespoons dried shredded coconut
1 tablespoon fresh (or bottled in brine)
 green peppercorns

1 Heat the sunflower oil in a heavy pan and fry the cumin seeds and crushed pepper for 1 minute. Add the onion and fry until soft, for about 4–5 minutes.

2 Add the ginger-garlic paste and the red chiles and stir a couple of times.

3 Tip in the turmeric and the potatoes. Season with salt. Mix well and pour in a few tablespoons of hot water to prevent the potatoes from sticking. Cover and cook until the potatoes hold their shape but are tender. Stir in the coconut, heat through, and serve at once with the green peppercorns sprinkled on top.

eggplants with tamarind and cashews
bagare baingan

Although this recipe looks a bit complicated, it is possibly one of the first things I learned to make entirely on my own. The results were so successful that it has remained a firm favorite. I sometimes like to add a bit of jaggery (palm sugar) for a hint of sweetness. Choose small eggplants that have virtually no seeds for the best flavor.

Serves: 4
Preparation time: 15 minutes
Cooking time: 40 minutes

2 tablespoons sunflower oil
4 dried red chiles, broken in half and
 seeds shaken out
15 cashews
1 tablespoon coriander seeds
1 medium onion, sliced
$^1/_4$ cup freshly grated or
 dried, shredded coconut
1 tablespoon white sesame seeds
1 tablespoon ginger-garlic paste (page 11)
Salt, to taste
$^1/_2$ teaspoon turmeric
11 ounces small eggplants
1 teaspoon tamarind concentrate, diluted in
 $^2/_3$ cup hot water
1 tablespoon soft brown sugar

1 Heat half the oil in a heavy pan and fry the chiles, cashews, and coriander seeds. In a few seconds, add the onion. Stir often and, when the onion turns golden brown, add the coconut and sesame seeds.

2 When the coconut starts to turn brown, add the ginger-garlic paste and mix well. Remove from the heat, cool slightly, and whizz in a blender with a few tablespoons of water to make a fine paste. Season the paste with salt, stir in the turmeric, and set aside.

3 Keeping the stem intact, slit the eggplants twice in a cross nearly all the way to the stem. Stuff each eggplant with the reserved spice paste. If there is some left over, reserve this for the sauce.

4 Heat the remaining oil in a heavy pan or kadhai. Place the stuffed eggplants into the pan and fry for a couple of minutes. Add the extra stuffing if available.

5 Pour in the tamarind water, sprinkle in the sugar, and bring to a boil. Reduce the heat and simmer until the eggplants are cooked through. Serve hot with Lemon Rice with Cashews and Peanuts (page 120), and with a sprinkling of chopped cilantro leaves, if you like.

sweet and sour okra
kodel

Okra is a difficult vegetable to cook if you don't know a few tricks. Adding water to it will make it slimier but adding an acid, in this case the tamarind, will help get rid of the slime. The sauce should be thick, almost the consistency of custard. You can substitute the okra for any soft vegetable such as pumpkin or doodhi.

Serves: 4
Preparation time: 15 minutes
Cooking time: 40 minutes

2 tablespoons sunflower oil
3 dried red chiles, broken in half and
  seeds shaken out
1/2 teaspoon cumin seeds
6 black peppercorns
1 teaspoon white poppy seeds
1/2 teaspoon fenugreek seeds
1 medium onion, sliced
5 tablespoons freshly grated or
  dried, shredded coconut
1/2 teaspoon black mustard seeds
11 ounces okra, washed, dried, and sliced
  into long strips (about 3–3 1/2 cups)
1 tablespoon tamarind concentrate, diluted in
  6 tablespoons water
2 tablespoons soft brown sugar
Salt, to taste

1 Heat half the oil in a heavy pan and fry the chiles, cumin seeds, peppercorns, poppy seeds, and fenugreek seeds until they start to change color.

2 Add the onion and fry until slightly brown. Tip in the coconut and continue frying over low heat until the coconut turns brown. Remove from the heat, cool slightly, and whizz in a blender with a few tablespoons of water to make a fine paste. Set aside.

3 Heat the remaining oil in a kadhai or heavy pan and add the mustard seeds. When they pop, add the okra and stir for a couple of minutes.

4 Pour in the tamarind water and add the sugar and salt. Add the reserved paste and bring to a boil. Reduce the heat and simmer for 7–8 minutes until the okra is cooked. Serve hot with rice.

cauliflower with fenugreek
cauliflower sukke

This recipe is from the Saraswat Brahmin community of Karnataka, to which my mother belongs. The final dish should be fairly dry, the vegetables coated with the sauce rather than swimming in it. Jaggery (palm sugar) is not easily available everywhere outside India and, although it adds a thicker consistency and a deeper taste, I find that soft brown sugar is acceptable.

Serves: 4
Preparation time: 15 minutes
Cooking time: 40 minutes

2 tablespoons sunflower oil
1 teaspoon split black lentils (urad dal)
1 teaspoon coriander seeds
5 dried red chiles
1/4 cup freshly grated or dried,
  shredded coconut
1 teaspoon tamarind concentrate, diluted in
  6 tablespoons water
1/2 teaspoon turmeric
1 medium onion, sliced
11 ounces cauliflower, cut into florets
  (about 4 cups)
Salt, to taste
1/2 teaspoon jaggery or soft brown sugar

1 Heat half the oil in a heavy pan and fry the lentils, coriander seeds, and chiles until they start to change color.

2 Add the coconut and fry until brown, stirring frequently to prevent it from sticking. Remove from the heat, cool slightly, and whizz in a blender with a few tablespoons of water and the tamarind, to make a fine paste of pouring consistency. Mix in the turmeric and set aside.

3 Heat the remaining oil in a kadhai or heavy pan and add the onion. Stir until it browns and add the cauliflower. Season with salt, add the sugar, and pour in the reserved spice paste.

4 Bring to a boil, reduce the heat, and cook until the cauliflower is just tender. Serve with Coconut-flavored Rice (page 119).

bamboo shoots in coconut milk
kirla ghassi

Manglore is on the western coast of India and has produced a distinctive coconut-based cuisine that is popular all over India. This is a classic curry with tender bamboo shoots, which are quite common in this region and are cooked on festive days. Fresh bamboo shoots are prepared by peeling off the outer skin and slicing off the tough parts to get to the soft core, which is soaked for 48 hours, changing the water every 12 hours. I prefer to use canned bamboo shoots!

Serves: 4
Preparation time: 15 minutes
Cooking time: 25 minutes

3 tablespoons sunflower oil
1 teaspoon coriander seeds
5 ounces dried, shredded coconut
  (about 2 cups)
1/2 teaspoon garam masala
1 teaspoon tamarind concentrate, diluted in
  1/4 cup water
1/4 teaspoon chili powder
1/4 teaspoon turmeric
1 x 14-ounce can bamboo shoots, drained
Salt, to taste
2/3 cup coconut milk
7–8 curry leaves

1 Heat half the oil in a heavy pan and add the coriander seeds and coconut. Stir until brown.

2 Remove from the heat and add the garam masala and the tamarind. Cool slightly and whizz to a fine paste in a blender. Set aside.

3 Heat the remaining oil in a wok and add the chili and turmeric. Add the bamboo shoots and salt.

4 Tip in the reserved coconut mixture, add a little water, and bring to a boil. Pour in the coconut milk and add the curry leaves; simmer for 2–3 minutes and remove from the heat. Serve hot but without boiling, as the coconut milk may curdle.

stir-fried green tomatoes
pacha thakali kari

Firm and tangy green tomatoes are used in south Indian cookery. They are sometimes combined with potatoes or peanuts and used in wedding feasts or on the day of Kerala's favorite festival, Onam. Traditionally a couple of teaspoons of coconut oil are poured onto this dish before serving, to add a unique flavor, but I have left this out to make a healthier version of the recipe.

Serves: 4
Preparation time: 10 minutes
Cooking time: 20 minutes

2 tablespoons sunflower oil
2 fresh green chiles, chopped
1 large onion, finely chopped
Large pinch of asafetida
6 curry leaves
11 ounces green tomatoes (about 2 medium
  or 3 small), cubed
Salt, to taste
2 tablespoons dried, shredded coconut

1 Heat the oil in a heavy pan or kadhai and fry the green chiles and onion until soft.

2 Add the asafetida, curry leaves, and tomatoes. Season with salt and cook over high heat for a couple of minutes. Reduce the heat and add a few tablespoons of water. Simmer for 10 minutes.

3 Remove from the heat, stir in the coconut, and serve hot with rice and Sambhar (page 138).

stir-fried plantain with garlic
vazhakai thoran

Plantains are popular in south Indian cooking, especially in Kerala. They are a type of banana with quite firm flesh and a tough skin. They should be cooked. The skin can be easily scraped off with a peeler. The flesh is slightly sticky and tastes like a banana-flavored potato when cooked. This tastes much better with fresh coconut so do use it if you can.

Serves: 4
Preparation time: 15 minutes
Cooking time: 30 minutes

2 fresh green chiles
6 tablespoons freshly grated or
  dried, shredded coconut
2 cloves garlic, chopped
11 ounces plantains (about 2 small)
Salt, to taste
1/2 teaspoon turmeric
7 curry leaves
1 tablespoon sunflower oil
1 medium onion, sliced

1 Put the chiles, coconut, and garlic into a blender, add a few tablespoons of water, and grind to a fine paste. Set aside.

2 Peel the plantains with a potato peeler and chop into small pieces. Put them into a saucepan with 1¼ cups of water, some salt, and the turmeric, and bring to a boil. Reduce the heat, add the reserved coconut paste and curry leaves, and simmer for 10–12 minutes until the plantains are cooked through and just tender. Heat the oil in a small saucepan and fry the onion until brown. Pour it over the plantains and serve hot.

lentil pancakes
dosas

A fabulous dish from south India and one that is served at any time of the day. My own family is part south Indian and I have had dosas for breakfast, as a teatime snack, and for dinner. They are served with a variety of chutneys made of coconut, tangy unripe mangoes, red chiles, or curry leaves. They can also be served with a spicy potato filling and these are called "masala dosas." Please do not be put off by the long preparation time. The final dish is worth it and all it needs is a little bit of pre-planning!

Serves: 4
Preparation time: 15 minutes + overnight
  soaking + 2 hours, fermenting time
Cooking time: 25 minutes

1¹/2 **cups basmati rice or broken basmati rice**
  (available at Indian grocery stores and
  cheaper than normal basmati rice)
³/4 **cup skinless split black lentils**
Salt, to taste
Sunflower oil for shallow frying

1 Soak the rice and the lentils separately in plenty of water, preferably overnight or at least for 4 hours. Drain away the water and grind them separately in a blender, adding a little water as necessary, until you get 2 smooth, thick batters. Combine these batters and season with salt. Let them ferment in a warm place for a couple of hours.

2 Heat an iron griddle or a nonstick pan and pour in 1 teaspoonful oil.

3 Stir the batter well and pour a ladleful of it into the center of the pan. Spread the mixture quickly making a neat, small circle.

4 Drizzle a few drops of oil around the edges of the pancake. Reduce the heat, cover the pan, and cook for a few seconds. Turn the pancake over with a spatula and cook the other side. You might have to discard the first pancake as it might be sticky and irregular in shape. Don't worry. The first one seems to season the pan for those to follow!

5 Continue similarly for the rest of the pancakes, keeping them warm as you go along, and serve at once.

steamed rice cakes
idlis

Idlis are served for breakfast or teatime over most of south India. These cakes are soft, fluffy, and very nutritious. The mixture of lentils and rice means that they have proteins and carbohydrates. My little daughter loves to eat them with a pat of butter. Make variations by adding vegetables or spices to the batter: I love green beans and crushed black pepper.

Serves: 4
Preparation time: 20 minutes + overnight
  soaking + 8 hours fermenting time
Cooking time: 15 minutes

1¹/2 **cups basmati rice or broken basmati rice**
  (available at Indian grocery stores)
¹/2 **cup skinless split black lentils**
Salt, to taste

1 Soak the rice and the lentils separately in plenty of water overnight. Drain and grind them separately in a blender, adding fresh water as necessary, to make thick, pouring batter. (If you grind them together, the batter will not be smooth enough.) Mix the two batters together and add the salt. Let them ferment in a warm place for about 8 hours.

2 Pour the batter into little metal bowls (that can be put into a steamer) or an egg poacher, and steam the cakes for 15 minutes.

3 To serve, remove each cake by sliding a sharp knife under it and lifting. Set aside and keep warm. Repeat this process until all the batter is used up. Serve warm with Coconut Chutney (page 131) and Sambhar (page 138).

semolina pancake with onion and cilantro
rava uttappam

South Indians are skillful at making all sorts of pancakes. These are eaten with chutneys, sweet preserves, or curries. Uttappam is a kind of dosa and can also be flavored with tomatoes or grated cheese as well as onions. Some dosas, like this one, can be made in advance for convenience and reheated, but I always think there is nothing quite like eating pancakes hot from the pan!

Serves: 4
Preparation time: 10 minutes
Cooking time: 25 minutes

1 medium onion, finely chopped
1 heaping cup coarse semolina
Pinch of turmeric
Salt, to taste
Handful of cilantro leaves, finely chopped
2 fresh green chiles, finely chopped
Sunflower oil for shallow frying

1 Combine the onion, semolina, turmeric, salt, cilantro, and chiles in a mixing bowl. Pour in enough cold water to make a batter of pouring consistency, almost like thick custard.

2 Heat 1 tablespoon of oil in a large pan. Pour a ladleful of the batter into the center and spread it in quick circles to form a flattish disc about 4 inches in diameter. Cover the pan and let the pancake cook in its steam.

3 Flip the pancake over when the underside has turned golden and spotted. Cook the other side by dotting the edges with some oil and covering the pan. Keep warm.

4 Make all the pancakes similarly and serve hot with Coconut Chutney (page 131).

hyderabadi vegetable biryani
tahiri

There is a refined biryani that symbolizes the Islamic influence on south Indian food. Built around 1580, the city of Hyderabad in Andhra Pradesh was called Bhagnagar, after the beautiful Bhagmati who was the beloved of the Nawab. She later changed her name to Hyder Mahal and the city was renamed after her. This dish is a festive one that needs time and patience but makes a great Sunday feast!

Serves: 4
Preparation time: 25 minutes
Cooking time: 40 minutes

1¹/2 cups basmati rice, washed and drained
Sunflower oil for deep-frying
11 ounces mixed vegetables—potatoes, eggplant, cauliflower (about 3–4 cups), cut into small pieces
1 large onion, finely sliced
1 teaspoon raisins
2 teaspoons ginger-garlic paste (page 11)
2 fresh green chiles, finely chopped
¹/2 teaspoon turmeric
1 teaspoon garam masala
¹/2 cup plain yogurt
Salt, to taste
Juice of 1 lemon
Handful of cilantro and mint leaves, chopped
2 tablespoons ghee

1 Put the rice with 3 cups of hot water in a saucepan and bring to a boil. Reduce the heat, stir, cover, and simmer for 10 minutes until done. Set aside.

2 Heat the oil in a deep frying pan and deep-fry the vegetables until cooked, first the cauliflower and potatoes, then the eggplant. Drain and set aside.

3 Add half the onion and fry until dark brown, drain and set aside. Fry the raisins for 1 minute, drain, and reserve them separately.

4 In a large clean pot, heat 2 tablespoons of oil and fry the rest of the onion until golden brown. Add the ginger-garlic paste, chiles, turmeric, and garam masala. Gently stir in the fried vegetables, yogurt, and salt and simmer for 10 minutes.

5 Now start to assemble the tahiri. In an ovenproof serving dish, put one layer of rice and one of the vegetable mixture. Sprinkle some lemon juice over it, along with some of the cilantro and mint leaves.

6 Begin with the next layer of rice and keep going till you have a layer of rice at the top. Drizzle the ghee over it and serve hot, garnished with the fried onions, raisins, and the remaining cilantro and mint leaves.

7 Keep it warm in a 350°F oven until you are ready to serve.

coconut-flavored rice
thengai sadam

A soft and gentle dish that makes a perfect summer meal. The juiciness of fresh coconut is vital and therefore it cannot be substituted with dried coconut. In India, the coconut is given a place of honor at ceremonies such as weddings and rituals. It is also called shriphal or the fruit of the gods and is sometimes used as a symbol of Divinity.

Serves: 4
Preparation time: 15 minutes
Cooking time: 30 minutes

1¹/2 cups basmati rice, washed and drained
2 tablespoons sunflower oil
1 teaspoon black mustard seeds
2 tablespoons cashews
1 teaspoon chopped fresh green chiles
2 teaspoons split black lentils (urad dal), soaked in water for 15 minutes and drained
Large pinch of asafetida
7 curry leaves
6 ounces freshly grated coconut (about 1–1¹/2 cups)
Salt, to taste

1 Put the rice with 3 cups of hot water in a pan and bring to a boil. Reduce the heat, stir, cover, and simmer for 10 minutes until cooked. Set aside.

2 Heat the oil and fry the mustard seeds. When they pop, add the cashews, chiles, lentils, asafetida, and curry leaves. Fry for 1 minute, add the coconut, and stir until the color begins turning golden, then season with salt. Remove from the heat and fold in the rice. Serve with Kholombo Powder (page 139) and Plantain Wafers (page 128).

lemon rice with cashews and peanuts
naranga choru

Rice is eaten in every south Indian household every single day. It generally features in two or three courses, first with spiced lentils and lastly with cool yogurt. I tend to keep lemon rice very lightly spiced although some versions are quite fiery. I like to believe that the rice should be fairly neutral so that it can be enjoyed with stronger dishes.

Serves: 4
Preparation time: 10 minutes
Cooking time: 25 minutes

$1^1/_2$ cups basmati rice, washed and drained
2 tablespoons sunflower oil
1 teaspoon black mustard seeds
6 curry leaves
1 teaspoon gram lentils (channa dal), soaked
  in water for 15 minutes and drained
10 cashews
2 tablespoons unsalted peanuts
1 teaspoon turmeric
3 tablespoons lemon juice
Salt, to taste

1 Put the rice and 3 cups of hot water in a heavy pan. Bring to a boil. Reduce the heat, stir, and cover. Simmer for 10 minutes until cooked. Set aside.

2 In a separate pan, heat the oil and fry the mustard seeds until they pop. Then add the curry leaves, lentils, cashews, and peanuts. Reduce the heat and, when the cashews are slightly brown, add the turmeric.

3 Remove from the heat at once and pour in the lemon juice and season with salt. Gently fold the rice into this mixture and serve hot.

tamarind rice
pulihodara

The tamarind pod is crescent-shaped and brown, with a thin, brittle shell. It contains a fleshy pulp held together by a fibrous husk. Within this pulp are squarish, dark brown, shiny seeds. The pulp, used as a flavoring for its sweet, sour, fruity aroma and taste, is dried along with the seeds and husk and sold in the form of little cakes. I use the concentrate for ease.

Serves: 4
Preparation time: 30 minutes
Cooking time: 30 minutes

$1^1/_2$ cups basmati rice, washed and drained
2 tablespoons sunflower oil
$^1/_2$ teaspoon black mustard seeds
$^1/_4$ teaspoon fenugreek seeds
Large pinch of asafetida
4 dried red chiles, seeded and crumbled
1 teaspoon gram lentils (channa dal)
2 teaspoons cashews
10 curry leaves
1 tablespoon tamarind concentrate, diluted in
  6 tablespoons water
Salt, to taste

1 Put the rice with 3 cups of hot water in a pan and bring to a boil. Reduce the heat, stir, cover, and simmer for 10 minutes until cooked. Set aside.

2 Heat the oil in a heavy pan and fry the mustard seeds, fenugreek seeds, asafetida, chiles, lentils, cashews, and curry leaves.

3 Stir in the tamarind and salt, cooking until the tamarind is thick and the paste is well blended. Fold in the rice and serve hot.

flaked rice with potatoes
batate pohe

Serves: 4
Preparation time: 20 minutes
Cooking time: 15 minutes

$2^3/_4$ cups Indian rice flakes (pawa)
1 teaspoon turmeric
Salt, to taste
1 teaspoon sugar
1 tablespoon sunflower oil
1 teaspoon black mustard seeds
$^1/_2$ teaspoon cumin seeds
Large pinch of asafetida
2 fresh green chiles, finely chopped
12 curry leaves
1 medium potato, peeled, cubed, and boiled
2 teaspoons lemon juice
Few cilantro leaves, chopped
2 tablespoons freshly grated
  or diced, shredded coconut

1 Soak the rice flakes in water for 5 minutes and drain. Then mix the rice, turmeric, salt, and sugar together gently. Set aside.

2 Heat the oil in a pan and add the mustard seeds. When they crackle, add the cumin, asafetida, chiles, and curry leaves.

3 Fry for 1 minute and stir in the potatoes. Add the flaked rice. Mix well. Reduce the heat, sprinkle in about 4 tablespoons of water, cover, and simmer for about 10 minutes. Drizzle in the lemon juice. The potatoes will become slightly mushy, which will give a creamy texture to the dish.

4 Serve hot, garnished with the cilantro and coconut.

spiced lentils with shallots
vengai sambhar

The aroma of sambhar reminds me of the Temple of Meenakshi, the Goddess with the fish-shaped eyes, in south India. After the ritual worship, streams of devotees are served a simple meal of rice, sambhar, ghee, and sweets. Sambhar is made every day in traditional south Indian homes, especially in Tamil Nadu. The recipe for Sambhar Powder, the spice mix that flavors this dish, is given on page 138.

Serves: 4
Preparation time: 15 minutes + 30 minutes
  soaking time
Cooking time: 40 minutes

$1^2/_3$ cups split yellow lentils (toor dal),
  soaked in water for 30 minutes and drained
$3^1/_4$ cups water
12 shallots, peeled
Salt
1 teaspoon turmeric
2 tablespoons sunflower oil
1 teaspoon black mustard seeds
1 teaspoon cumin seeds
12 curry leaves
Large pinch of asafetida
1 teaspoon tamarind concentrate, diluted in
  6 tablespoons water
2 teaspoons sambhar powder (page 138)
2 tablespoons chopped cilantro leaves

1 Put the lentils and the water in a heavy pan and bring to a boil. Reduce the heat and simmer, skimming off the scum that rises to the top. When the lentils are nearly tender, add the shallots and simmer until they are just softening. The lentils are done when they get mushy.

2 Add the salt and turmeric. Mix well, remove from the heat, and set aside.

3 Heat the oil in a small pan and add the mustard seeds. When they crackle, add the cumin seeds, curry leaves, and asafetida, then the tamarind, and cook over low heat until thick and bubbly.

4 Add the sambhar powder and cook for 1 minute. Pour the mixture over the lentils and stir. Swirl a few tablespoons of water in the pan to gather all the tamarind and spices and pour it into the lentils. Serve hot, garnished with the cilantro.

lentil soup with tamarind and garlic rasam

Rasam is a close relative of sambhar but it is thinner and is therefore often served as a spicy soup. Try it on cold winter nights! It is also eaten with boiled rice, as a second course after rice and sambhar. You could add lemon juice instead of the tamarind to make lemon rasam, in which case, add the lemon juice at the end, after taking the rasam off the heat (step 3).

Serves: 4
Preparation time: 15 minutes + 15 minutes soaking time
Cooking time: 30 minutes

1/4 cup split yellow lentils (toor dal), soaked for 15 minutes and drained
3 1/4 cups water
Salt, to taste
1 teaspoon jaggery or soft brown sugar
2 tablespoons sunflower oil
1/2 teaspoon black mustard seeds
1/2 teaspoon cumin seeds
Large pinch of asafetida
10 curry leaves
4 cloves garlic, peeled and bruised
1 teaspoon tamarind concentrate, diluted in 6 tablespoons water
1 teaspoon sambhar powder (page 138)
1 teaspoon turmeric
2 tablespoons chopped cilantro leaves

1 Put the lentils and the water in a heavy pan, bring to a boil, and simmer until mushy, skimming the scum off the surface from time to time. Add the salt and the jaggery, mixing until they dissolve.

2 Heat the oil in a separate pan and add the mustard seeds. When they crackle, add the cumin, asafetida, curry leaves, and the whole cloves of garlic. Fry for 1 minute, then add the tamarind and cook until it becomes thick and bubbly. Stir in the spice powders.

3 Pour the lentils into the tamarind mixture, bring to a boil and remove from the heat. Stir gently and serve hot with the cilantro.

green lentil pancake
pessaratu

This is a specialty of Andhra Pradesh and is not made in other southern states. It is a classic dish and nutritious. There is a story that there was once a great famine in Andhra Pradesh and nothing but chiles could be grown and this is why the cooking here is hot and spicy. Every meal is served with ghee to temper the heat of the chiles, most of which come from a place called Guntur. Soaking the chiles makes them soft enough to blend into a paste.

Serves: 4
Preparation time: 15 minutes + 4 hours
  soaking time
Cooking time: 30 minutes

3/4 cup split green lentils (split mung lentils
  with the green skin on)
1 teaspoon cumin seeds
2 fresh green chiles, chopped
2 dried red chiles, seeds shaken out,
  soaked in a little water for 15 minutes
  and drained
1 medium onion, finely chopped
Few cilantro leaves, finely chopped
Salt, to taste
Sunflower oil for frying

1 Soak the lentils in plenty of water for 4 hours. Drain and grind them to a smooth paste in a blender, along with the cumin seeds, green and red chiles, and enough fresh water to achieve pouring consistency.

2 Stir in the onion and cilantro leaves and season with salt.

3 Heat a flat griddle or nonstick frying pan and put a ladleful of the batter at the center. Spread with the back of a spoon to make a disc about 4 inches in diameter and dot the edges with oil. When the underside is cooked, turn it over to cook the other side.

4 Remove from the heat and continue in the same fashion with the rest of the batter. Pessaratu are served with butter and jaggery or soft brown sugar.

smoky lentils
with tomato
tomato kholombo

This dish is made by the Saraswat community of Karnataka. Chopped eggplant or pumpkin can be substituted for the tomato, in which case, cook the vegetables separately and add to the lentils with the tamarind. This dish tastes better a day after you make it.

Serves: 4
Preparation time: 15 minutes
Cooking time: 50 minutes

1 cup split red lentils (masoor dal), washed
  and drained
Salt, to taste
1 teaspoon tamarind concentrate, diluted in
  4 teaspoons water
3 ripe tomatoes, chopped
1 teaspoon kholombo powder (page 139)
2 tablespoons sunflower oil
1/2 teaspoon black mustard seeds
4 dried red chiles, seeded and crumbled
Large pinch of asafetida
12 curry leaves

1 Put the lentils and 2 cups of hot water into a pan and bring to a boil. Reduce the heat and simmer until the lentils are mushy, for about 30 minutes.

2 Add the salt, tamarind, tomatoes, and kholombo powder, and simmer for a couple of minutes, then remove from the heat and set aside.

3 Heat the oil in a small saucepan and add the mustard seeds. When they crackle, add the chiles, asafetida, and curry leaves. Pour this over the lentils. Mix well and serve with rice and a hot relish.

lima beans in garlic and coconut
aurey bendi

This recipe is from the Saraswat community of Goa. It looks quite red and fiery but it is almost creamy and spicy rather than hot. A native spice berry called "tirphal" which is extremely fragrant and is slightly bitter is used in Goa, and when it is not flavored with this spice, garlic is added as the main flavoring. It is eaten with plain rice. You can use other beans such as black-eyed peas, which work well in this recipe.

Serves: 4
Preparation time: 15 minutes
Cooking time: 20 minutes

1 cup freshly grated or dried shredded coconut
4 dried red chiles, seeded, stems
  removed, soaked in a little water
2 teaspoons tamarind concentrate, diluted in
  3 tablespoons water
12-ounce can lima beans, drained
Salt, to taste
2 teaspoons sunflower oil
2 cloves garlic, sliced

1 Grind the coconut, red chiles, and tamarind in a blender, adding water as needed to make a very fine paste.

2 In a large pan, combine the beans and the coconut paste and add enough water to make a pouring consistency. Bring to a boil. Season with salt, reduce the heat and simmer for a few minutes. Remove from the heat and set aside.

3 Heat the oil in a small saucepan. Add the garlic and fry for 1 minute until it just starts to turn golden and a delicious aroma fills the air! Pour it over the bean curry. Stir and serve hot.

lentils with spinach
soppu palya

Serves: 4
Preparation time: 15 minutes
Cooking time: 60 minutes

3/4 cup yellow lentils (toor dal), washed
3 large handfuls spinach, chopped
2 tablespoons sunflower oil
1 teaspoon coriander seeds
3 dried red chiles
1/4 cup freshly grated coconut
1 teaspoon tamarind concentrate, diluted in
  1/4 cup water
1/2 teaspoon turmeric
Salt, to taste
1 medium onion, sliced

1 Put the lentils and 1 1/2 cups of hot water into a saucepan and bring to a boil. Reduce the heat and simmer until the lentils are mushy, for about 35 minutes.

2 In the meantime, place the spinach in a pot along with a little hot water and heat it for a couple of minutes. Add it to the lentils.

3 In a separate pan, heat half the oil and fry the coriander seeds until they turn dark, then add the chiles and the coconut. Reduce the heat and stir for a couple of minutes. Remove from the heat, let it cool slightly, then tip it into a blender along with the tamarind and few tablespoons of water and blend until you get a fine paste.

4 Add this to the lentils, along with the turmeric and salt.

5 Heat the remaining oil in a small saucepan and fry the onions until golden, then add them to the lentils. Reheat thoroughly and serve hot with rice.

lentil fritters in sweet yogurt
thayir vadai

The fritters in this recipe can be made with a variety of lentils, but I often choose the split yellow mung ones because they are quick to cook and very easy to digest. They need to be soaked so that they become soft enough to blend into a batter. Versions of this recipe are popular in north India but there no sugar is added, and the curry leaves are substituted with cilantro leaves.

Serves: 4
Preparation time: 20 minutes + 3 hours
  soaking time
Cooking time: 25 minutes

3/4 cup split yellow mung lentils, washed
  and drained
Salt, to taste
Sunflower oil for deep-frying
1 1/2 cups plain yogurt
2 teaspoons sugar
1 teaspoon black mustard seeds
1/2 teaspoon cumin seeds
3 large dried red chiles, seeds shaken out
7 curry leaves

1 Soak the mung lentils in plenty of water for at least 3 hours. Drain off the water and grind the lentils in a blender with a few tablespoons of fresh water. The result should be a smooth paste with no grains in it, the consistency of thick custard. Season with salt and set aside.

2 Heat the oil in a deep pot or wok. When it is nearly smoking, drop in a tiny ball of the lentil batter. It should rise quickly to the top. Reduce the heat slightly and gently drop a few tablespoons of the batter into the oil. Turn them around a few times to brown them evenly. Don't hurry them along or they will brown on the outside but remain uncooked in the middle.

3 When the first batch is done, use a slotted spoon to scoop out the fritters. Drain them on paper towels. Cook the remaining fritters in the same way.

4 In another bowl, whisk together the yogurt, some salt, and the sugar.

5 Heat a tablespoon of oil in a small saucepan and fry the mustard seeds until they pop. Add the cumin seeds, red chiles, and curry leaves and then pour this tempering along with the oil into the seasoned yogurt.

6 Just before serving, add the fritters to the yogurt. Some cooks dip them in water, squeeze them dry, and then add them to the yogurt to soften them and help them absorb the yogurt, but if you like the fritters crisp, add them directly into the yogurt. Serve cool.

plantain wafers
vazhaikkai varuval

No south Indian meal is complete without some fried accompaniment. Sometimes this might be store-bought potato chips or a variety of poppadoms made of lentils and rice flour. I love these wafers for their crisp texture and divine taste. In the south, they are often fried in coconut oil. It is easiest to peel the plantain with a potato peeler.

Serves: 4
Preparation time: 15 minutes
Cooking time: 20 minutes

2 plantains, peeled and sliced
1/4 teaspoon turmeric
1/4 teaspoon chili powder
Salt, to taste
2 tablespoons rice flour
Sunflower oil for deep-frying

1 Mix the plantains and spices together and season with salt. Sprinkle in the rice flour and see that each slice is well coated.

2 Heat the oil in a deep pot or wok and, when nearly smoking, take the plantain slices at a time, until golden. Serve at once or keep warm.

coconut chutney
thengai thuvaiyal

This is the most versatile chutney made throughout south India and is served with pancakes, rice, fried accompaniments, or breads. It makes a great sandwich filler, too! Dried coconut cannot be used here as the chutney must be fragrant with the smell of fresh coconut. Jaggery is unrefined palm sugar and tastes quite toffee-like. Brown sugar can be substituted.

Serves: 4
Preparation time: 15 minutes
Cooking time: 2 minutes

2 teaspoons sunflower oil
3 dried red chiles
1 teaspoon split black lentils (urad dal)
Pinch of asafetida
$1/2$ cup freshly grated coconut
1 teaspoon tamarind concentrate, diluted in
   $1/4$ cup water
1 teaspoon jaggery or soft brown sugar
Salt, to taste
1 teaspoon black mustard seeds

1 Heat half the oil in a pan and fry the red chiles, lentils, and asafetida until the lentils turn brown. Remove from the heat and mix in the coconut.

2 Combine with the tamarind, the jaggery or sugar, and the salt in a blender and add enough water to whizz it into a thick, smooth paste. Pour into a serving dish.

3 Heat the remaining oil in a small saucepan and fry the mustard seeds until they pop, then pour them into the chutney. Serve cold.

fresh ginger and yogurt raita
inji pachadi

Ginger is often seen in festive feasts where the food is first offered to the gods. Its fragrance is especially prized along with its healing properties and it is served in many teas, salads, and desserts. Look for shiny, fine skinnned ginger when buying it. It should snap easily, which means it is juicy and fresh. As it gets older it turns leathery, dry, and fibrous.

Serves: 4
Preparation time: 15 minutes
Cooking time: 2 minutes

1 fresh green chile, finely chopped
2 tablespoons fresh peeled ginger, chopped
$1/4$ cup freshly grated or
   dried, shredded coconut
Salt, to taste
$3/4$ cup plain yogurt, beaten
1 tablespoon raisins
1 teaspoon sunflower oil
$1/2$ teaspoon black mustard seeds

1 Whizz the chile, ginger, and coconut in a blender along with some water to make a smooth paste, and season it with salt.

2 Mix in the yogurt and raisins and pour into a serving dish.

3 Heat the oil in a small saucepan and fry the mustard seeds until they pop. Pour them into the raita and mix gently. Serve as an accompaniment with Idlis (page 114) or Dosa (page 114).

jewish potatoes
alu mukkadah

The Jews in south India live mainly in Cochin in Kerala though there are few families left now. They follow the rules of their religion but, in deference to local Hindu customs, many of them do not eat beef. This recipe is extremely easy to make. It can be made with roasting potatoes as well but I love the baby ones that cook so quickly.

Serves: 4
Preparation time: 10 minutes
Cooking time: 20 minutes

11 ounces new potatoes (about 2–2$1/2$ cups),
   washed and drained
Salt, to taste
$1/2$ teaspoon turmeric
2 tablespoons sunflower oil

1 Prick the potatoes with a fork and drop them into a pan of hot water to which salt and turmeric have been added. Bring to a boil.

2 Reduce the heat and gently simmer the potatoes until they are just tender. Drain.

3 Heat the oil in a large frying pan and add the potatoes. Stir-fry over low heat until golden and slightly crisp. Serve as an accompaniment with lentils and rice.

semolina and saffron pudding
rava kesari

This saffron-scented dessert is considered food for the gods and is often made on festive days. The saffron colors it orange and it is quite soft because of the ghee. Each region of India has its own version—flavored with pineapples, bananas, or nuts, and they are all truly delicious.

Serves: 4
Preparation time: 10 minutes
Cooking time: 20 minutes

²/₃ **cup ghee**
1 heaping cup semolina
³/₄ **cup sugar**
Large pinch of saffron
2 cups warm milk
Pinch of ground cardamom
2 teaspoons raisins

1 Heat the ghee in a heavy saucepan or kadhai and add the semolina, frying until it becomes pink and fragrant. Reduce the heat and add the sugar, and stir until it melts.

2 Mix the saffron into the milk and add it to the Kadhai. Stir rapidly to avoid lumps from forming; sometimes I use a whisk to get a smooth consistency.

3 Add the ground cardamom and the raisins and reduce the heat. Cover the pan and let it cook until the mixture is semi-dry and the semolina is cooked, for about 10–12 minutes. Serve warm.

stewed apricots with cream
qubani ka meetha

This is a very quick and simple party dessert to prepare at short notice. It is believed to have been the favorite of the erstwhile ruler of Hyderabad, the Nizam, who was so rich that he employed servants to wear his collection of pearls in order to keep them lustrous. In fact his pearl collection, it was said, could be spread out on the roof of his palace, from one end to the other. Hunza apricots cannot be substituted with orange ones.

Serves: 4
Preparation time: 10 minutes
Cooking time: 15 minutes

11 ounces hunza apricots
¹/₂ **cup sugar**
¹/₄ **cup heavy cream**
2 tablespoons crushed almonds

1 Soak the apricots overnight in plenty of water and drain. Pit the fruit and discard the seeds.

2 Put the apricots and sugar along with 2¹/₂ cups of water in a heavy saucepan and cook until tender and pulpy.

3 Put half the apricots in a blender and whizz a couple of times until they resemble a jam.

4 Spoon some of the whole apricots and some of the pulp into stemmed serving glasses. Drizzle the cream over them, sprinkle the almonds on top, and serve chilled. You can also serve the apricots with custard.

rich rice and coconut pudding
thengapal payasam

This dish conjures up rich south Indian feasts served at festivals such as Onam, which is celebrated in Kerala with grand boat races and colorful dances. Coconut grows everywhere along the southern coasts of India and is therefore used in each part of the meal—from soups to chutneys to desserts.

Serves: 4
Preparation time: 10 minutes
Cooking time: 1 hour

6 tablespoons basmati rice, washed and drained
2^1/$_2$ cups canned coconut milk
Sugar, to taste
Pinch of ground cardamom
Pinch of saffron
1 teaspoon ghee or sunflower oil
2 tablespoons cashews
2 tablespoons raisins

1 Put the rice and coconut milk into a heavy pan and bring to a boil. Reduce the heat and simmer for 40 minutes or so until the rice becomes mushy. Mash the rice roughly with a whisk while still on the burner.

2 Add the sugar, cardamom, and saffron, and stir well.

3 Heat the ghee or oil in a small saucepan and fry the cashews and raisins briefly. Mix gently into the rice and serve warm or cold.

goan coconut pastries
neureos

Christmas in Goa comes alive with every home cooking up feasts of entrées and desserts. Here is a dessert made from fresh coconut and local cashews. The pastries keep for about a week in an airtight container and last longer in the fridge.

Serves: 4
Preparation time: 20 minutes
Cooking time: 1 hour

2^1/$_3$ cups all-purpose flour, plus extra for flouring
4 tablespoons ghee or sunflower oil
Pinch of salt
^{3}/$_4$ cup sugar
1 cup freshly grated or dried, shredded coconut
2 tablespoons cashews, crushed
2 tablespoons raisins
Large pinch of ground cardamom
Sunflower oil for deep-frying

1 Mix the flour, half the ghee or oil, and the salt. Add just enough water to knead into a firm dough and set aside.

2 Heat the sugar and ^{3}/$_4$ cup of water in a heavy saucepan until a single thread syrup forms— it will form a 3-inch "thread" when dripped from the spoon. Then add the coconut, cashews, and raisins. As the mixture thickens, add the ground cardamon. Remove from the heat when the mixture has turned fairly dry and set aside.

3 Divide the dough into 8 small balls and roll each out into a disc about ^{1}/$_2$-inch thick, flouring the board as necessary.

4 Put a spoonful of the coconut filling in the middle, wet the edges, and fold it over to form a half-moon shape. Press down the edges and trim with a serrated cutter or knife.

5 Heat the oil in a deep frying pan. When nearly smoking hot, reduce the heat and deep-fry the pastries in batches, until golden. Drain and set aside. Serve cold or warm.

minty yogurt cooler
boorani

This refreshingly green drink from Hyderabad is a real thirst quencher. It goes well with a spicy main course as it helps neutralize the fiery effect of chiles and hot spices. Traditionally, Indian "rock salt" is used for this, which has a garlicky aroma that goes well with yogurt.

Serves: 4
Preparation time: 15 minutes
Cooking time: nil

1 teaspoon cumin seeds
Few mint leaves, chopped
Few cilantro leaves, chopped
1¹/₂ cups plain yogurt
1¹/₄ cups water
Salt, to taste

1 Roast the cumin in small frying pan and grind to a fine powder in a spice grinder or mortar and pestle. Set aside.

2 Grind the mint and cilantro leaves to a paste with some water in a blender.

3 Mix this green paste together with the yogurt, water, salt and ground cumin in a large mixing bowl and pour into individual serving glasses. Serve chilled.

herbal tea
kashaya

South Indians drink this healing tea throughout the day. The spices work to soothe and heal and the warmth of the drink calms the nerves and restores equilibrium. It is especially comforting if you have a cough, cold, or the flu, but it also makes an exceptional everyday drink to keep the throat well conditioned.

Serves: 4
Preparation time: 5 minutes
Cooking time: 15 minutes

3 tablespoons organic barley
¹/₂ teaspoon cumin seeds
Pinch of ground cardamom
¹/₄-inch piece of fresh ginger, bruised
2¹/₂ cups water
Jaggery or raw cane sugar, to taste

1 Put the barley, cumin, cardamom, ginger, and water in a large saucepan and bring to a boil.

2 Reduce the heat and simmer for 5 minutes. Strain and add sugar, if you like. Serve hot.

almond milk
badam doodh

Every Indian festival is associated with certain foods. Sharad Poornima or the full moon night in autumn is considered to be exceptionally beautiful, a night when the Mother Goddess showers her choicest blessings on her devotees. The occasion is celebrated with much feasting, usually on the flat roofs of houses or outdoors in gardens from where the moon can be appreciated. This milk drink is made to serve to visitors and friends.

Serves : 4
Preparation time: 15 minutes
Cooking time: nil

5 tablespoons almonds, soaked in water for 1 hour
2¹/₂ cups milk
Large pinch of ground cardamom
Honey or sugar, to taste

1 Blend the almonds along with their skins and a little of the milk, to form a fine paste in a blender. Don't worry if some nut pieces remain, they will add texture!

2 Stir the paste into the rest of the milk, sprinkle in the cardamom, sweeten to taste, and serve at room temperature.

sambhar powder

The special spice blend of south India is sambhar powder. Sambhar is a preparation of lentils and vegetables that is spiked with different spices and laced with coriander. Sambhar is eaten every day in Tamil Nadu as the lentils provide protein in a meat-free diet.

Sambhar powder is fine and has a strong, earthy, dry smell of roasted spices and lentils. Ready-made sambhar powder is available commercially but it is never quite as fragrant as the home-made one. However, if you get an authentic south Indian brand, it is often quite good. Make a small quantity although it will store for up to a year in a dry, airtight jar. There are many recipes for sambhar powder. Here is one:

1 teaspoon black mustard seeds
1 teaspoon fenugreek seeds
2 teaspoons cumin seeds
12 dried red chiles, seeded and
  stalks removed
1 teaspoon black peppercorns
1 teaspoon coriander seeds
1 teaspoon turmeric
1/4 teaspoon asafetida
1 tablespoon sunflower oil
3 teaspoons split black lentils (urad dal)
3 teaspoons split yellow lentils (toor dal)

kholombo powder

1 Heat a heavy pan and dry-roast the mustard, fenugreek, and cumin seeds, chiles, peppercorns, and coriander seeds. Keep the heat low and stir constantly to prevent burning. The seeds will crackle and fly out so beware!

2 Add the turmeric and asafetida, give the mixture a good stir, and remove from the heat. Transfer it to a bowl.

3 In the same pan, heat the oil and fry the lentils. When they turn dark, add to the roasted spices. Cool the mixture and grind in a blender until fine. When the mixture is completely cool, store in an airtight jar.

In the states of Maharashtra, Karnataka, and Goa along the western Konkan coast of India lives a community of people called the Konkani Saraswats to which my mother belongs. Saraswat or Konkani food is becoming increasingly popular in restaurants all over India because it is full of flavor and fragrance. As it is still relatively unknown, gourmets will have the pleasure of discovering its mysterious secrets.

Kholombo is a lentil dish not unlike sambhar with an aroma reminiscent of wood smoke that enhances the flavor of food, as grilling does meat on a barbecue. The taste is hot with a slightly bitter aftertaste. It is always used in conjunction with tamarind.

Commercially, kholombo powder is only available in very select Konkani shops and there are possibly only a few outside India. Therefore it is necessary to make the blend at home. Make small quantities and store in a dry, airtight container.

One of the best recipes I have found for kholombo powder is:

1 tablespoon sunflower oil
2 tablespoons split gram lentils (channa dal)
2 teaspoons coriander seeds
8 curry leaves
2 teaspoons cumin seeds
4 cloves
1 teaspoon black peppercorns
3/4-inch stick of cinnamon
3 tablespoons dried, shredded coconut

1 Heat the oil in a heavy saucepan and fry the lentils until they turn slightly dark.

2 Reduce the heat and add the coriander seeds, curry leaves, cumin seeds, cloves, peppercorns, and cinnamon, and fry for 1 minute.

3 Add the coconut and continue frying, stirring until the coconut has turned brown and the aroma is rich.

4 Remove from the pan and allow the mixture to cool. Grind to a powder in a blender. Store in an airtight jar and use within 3 months.

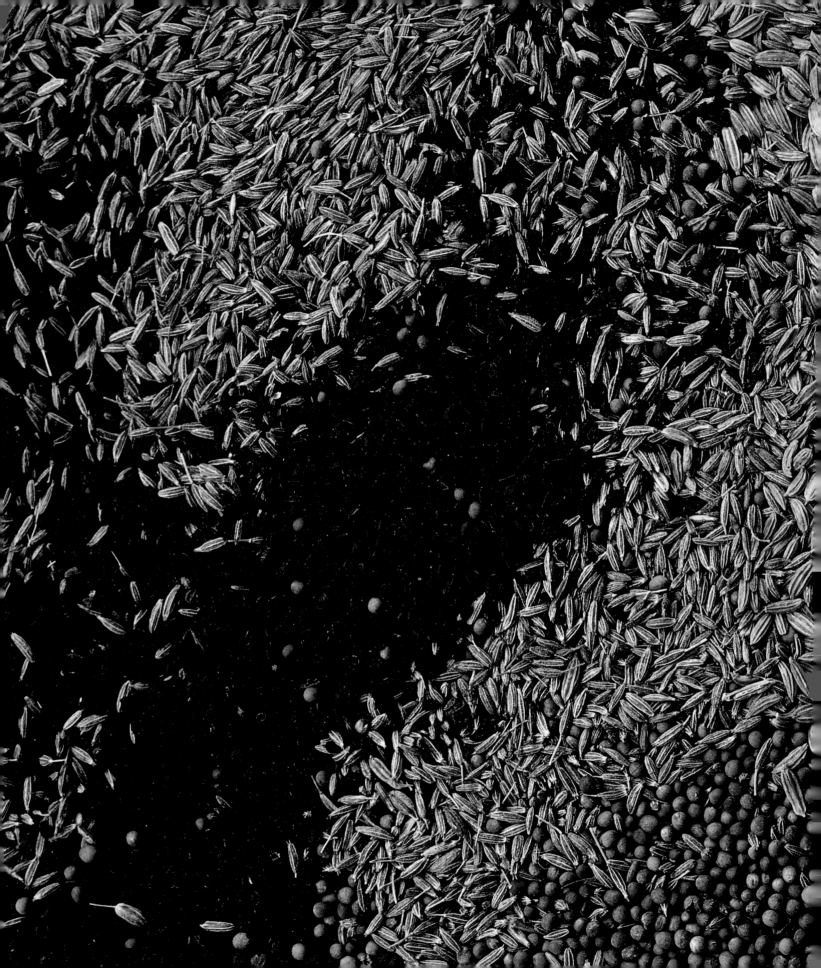

west bengal

The east is predominantly West Bengal and the cooking here is similar to that of the other eastern states such as Orissa. As in other parts of the country, availability of local ingredients has determined the flavor of the region. The many rivers and the fertile soil allow rice, mangoes and coconuts to grow and milk is available in plenty. Yogurt is spiced and ginger and mustard is used to flavor curries.

Although fish and meat are more popular, many people are, on the basis of their Hindu religion, vegetarian. Strict vegetarians will not eat even onion and garlic (see page 14), preferring instead a spice called asafetida that can be said to have a garlic-like aroma. Rice is eaten with all curries and the Bengalis grow one crop a year, leaving enough time to pursue what they love only second to eating—appreciation of the fine arts, namely music, painting, and literature.

Due to its proximity to the Mughal-influenced north of India, it is unsurprising that the Bengali Muslims have a cuisine with the best of kabobs and biryanis that are the pride of Mughlai cooking. Kolkatta, or Calcutta as it was formerly known, was the seat of the East India Company and the European traders introduced foods from their part of the world such as potatoes, chiles, and tomatoes. Bengali cooking soon adopted these and combined them with native ingredients.

West Bengal has a great vegetarian repertoire although the fish dishes are most famous. They will make ingenious use of parts of vegetables that most people would throw away, thus we have several chutneys made of peels or stalks of vegetables.

The use of spices is unique and a special blend called panch phoron or five spice mixture is used extensively. This is a mixture of cumin, fennel, fenugreek, kalonji (onion seeds), and black mustard. The five spice mixture is fried in a little oil and added to most dishes. Black mustard is ground to a paste to make fiery curries. But the unique feature of Bengali cooking is the repertoire of sweets. A mishti or sweet shop is seen on every street corner in Kolkatta and even in other cities of India. Syrupy rasmalai, milky sandesh, and a sweet yogurt called mishti dhoi all come from here.

broccoli with five spices
panch phodoner gobi

The Bengalis use this combination of five aromatic spices in many of their recipes. Black onion seeds are sold as "kalonji" in Indian stores. You can use any vegetable with this spice mixture for a quick stir-fry. I often use cauliflower or pumpkin.

Serves: 4
Preparation time: 10 minutes
Cooking time: 15 minutes

2 tablespoons sunflower oil
$1/2$ teaspoon cumin seeds
$1/2$ teaspoon fennel seeds
$1/2$ teaspoon fenugreek seeds
$1/2$ teaspoon black mustard seeds
$1/2$ teaspoon black onion seeds
$11/4$ pounds broccoli, cut into florets
1 teaspoon turmeric
1 teaspoon chili powder
Salt, to taste
1 teaspoon lemon juice

1 Heat the oil and add all the spice seeds.

2 As they pop and darken, add the broccoli, turmeric, and chili powder, and salt. Mix well and pour in a few tablespoons of water. Bring to a sizzle then reduce the heat and cook until the broccoli is tender but still holds its shape.

3 Raise the heat to get rid of any liquid that remains. Drizzle in the lemon juice and serve hot with Luchis (page 151).

baby eggplants in spiced yogurt
dhoi begun

There are many different kinds of eggplants available today. If you cannot find little ones, slice the large eggplants into discs and fry a few at a time in a shallow frying pan. Eggplants tend to absorb a lot of oil. In order to reduce this, make sure that the oil is very hot.

Serves: 4
Preparation time: 15 minutes
Cooking time: 35 minutes

11 ounces small eggplants, washed and slit down the middle
Salt
1 teaspoon turmeric
Sunflower oil for deep-frying
1 teaspoon cumin seeds
$1/2$ teaspoon chili powder
$3/4$ cup plain yogurt, beaten
$1/2$ teaspoon sugar

1 Rub the cut surface of the eggplants with salt and the turmeric. Heat the oil in a deep frying pan and deep-fry the eggplants. Drain and set aside.

2 Heat 1 tablespoon of oil in a small saucepan and add the cumin seeds. As they crackle, add the chili powder. Pour this into the yogurt. Add the sugar and a little salt and pour the spiced yogurt over the eggplants. Serve at once.

fried bitter gourds and potatoes
alu karela bhaja

Karela or bitter gourd is popular all over India as most people believe in the Ayurvedic advice that bitter tastes are healthy. Karela is also believed to help people who suffer from diabetes. In this recipe, the frying of the karela takes away some of the bitter taste although it is impossible to effectively diminish it by much. Serve this crunchy dish as a side to rice and lentils.

Serves: 4
Preparation time: 20 minutes
Cooking time: 35 minutes

2 tablespoons mustard oil or sunflower oil
$1/4$ teaspoon nigella seeds
$1/2$ teaspoon turmeric
11 ounces karela or bitter gourd, washed
  and cut into round slices (leave skin on)
11 ounces potatoes, peeled and cut into fries
  (about $2–2^1/2$ cups)
Salt, to taste
2 fresh green chiles, slit

1 Heat the oil in a large heavy saucepan or kadhai. When it is quite hot add the nigella seeds.

2 As they start to pop, add the turmeric and the bitter gourd. Stir for 1 minute. Then add the potatoes and stir for another minute.

3 Add salt and the green chiles. Cover the pan with an upside-down lid filled with water and cook over low heat until the vegetables are done. Serve hot.

bengali-style mixed vegetables
shukto

Every region in India has a recipe for mixed vegetables in spices; in fact many of these dishes are considered festive and offered to the gods. In order for them to be appropriate for this, they have to have a prescribed number of ingredients, especially vegetables. The best of seasonal vegetables are used for this purpose.

Serves: 4
Preparation time: 45 minutes
Cooking time: 45 minutes

3 tablespoons sunflower oil
3 ounces (about $1/2$–$3/4$ cup) each of:
karela or bitter gourd, sliced
potatoes, peeled and cut into chips
small eggplants, thickly sliced
fresh horseradish, thickly sliced
raw plantain, peeled and sliced
parwal or pointed gourds, peeled and sliced

grind to a fine paste with water as needed:
1-inch piece of fresh ginger, peeled
1 teaspoon black mustard seeds
2 teaspoons ground cumin
1 teaspoon chili powder
1 teaspoon turmeric

salt, to taste
1 teaspoon sugar
1 tablespoon ghee
1 teaspoon panch phoron (page 160)

1 Heat the oil in a large heavy saucepan and fry the karela until brown. Add the rest of the vegetables and keep frying until they all start to turn brown.

2 Add the ground ginger and spice mixture, and the salt and sugar and mix well. Pour in about $1/3$ cup of water and simmer until the vegetables are cooked.

3 Heat the ghee in a small pan and add the panch phoron. When it starts to pop, pour the entire mixture into the vegetables and stir gently.

4 Serve hot with Luchis (page 151) or rice.

potatoes with tamarind
alurdam

This sort of dish with baby potatoes exists all over north India and has filtered into the east. You can use larger potatoes, peeled and boiled, but the small ones taste better I think. The sauce can be made with other vegetables, too—try yams or eggplants.

Serves: 4
Preparation time: 10 minutes
Cooking time: 35 minutes

3 tablespoons sunflower oil
1/2 teaspoon black mustard seeds
Few curry leaves
1 tablespoon freshly grated peeled ginger
11 ounces new potatoes, boiled and drained
 (about 2–2¹/2 cups)
3 fresh green chiles, minced
1 teaspoon sugar
Salt, to taste
1 teaspoon tamarind concentrate, diluted in
 ¹/4 cup water

1 Heat the oil in a large heavy saucepan and fry the mustard seeds until they pop, then add the curry leaves and ginger.

2 Add the boiled potatoes and fry for a couple of minutes.

3 Add the chiles, sugar, salt, and tamarind. Reduce the heat and cook for about 5 minutes until a thick sauce forms. Serve hot with Luchis (page 151).

cabbage with five spices and ginger
bandhkophir chorchori

This recipe can also be made with cauliflower or red cabbage. I am often asked about which kind of mustard seeds are best to use in Indian cooking. Always use black mustard seeds in curries and stir-fries. Split mustard seeds, without their skin, are creamy in color and are used in savory relishes such as hot mango and hot chili.

Serves: 4
Preparation time: 20 minutes
Cooking time: 30 minutes

1 teaspoon black mustard seeds
2 teaspoons shredded peeled ginger
4 dried red chiles, seeded, soaked in
 water, and drained
3 tablespoons sunflower oil
1 large onion, finely sliced
11 ounces cabbage, finely shredded
 (about 5 cups)
Salt, to taste
2 teaspoons panch phoron (page 160)

1 Put the mustard seeds, ginger, and red chiles in a blender along with 5 tablespoons of water and whizz to a fine paste. Set aside.

2 Heat 2 tablespoons of the oil in a large pot and add the onion. Fry until golden, then add the cabbage. Stir-fry for a couple of minutes until just translucent and sprinkle in the ground spice mixture and salt.

3 Add ¹/4 cup of water and cook uncovered until the cabbage is done but still crisp. Remove from the heat and set aside.

4 Heat the remaining tablespoon of oil in a separate pan and add the panch phoron. When it crackles, pour the oil and the seeds over the cabbage. Mix well. Serve hot with Luchis (page 151) or with rice and Bengali Dal (page 153).

rice with ghee and spices
ghee bhaat

Although this is a simple-sounding recipe, every Bengali I know almost drools at the mention of ghee bhaat. This may be because it is very fragrant and goes well with so many lentils and vegetables. You could add vegetables to the rice such as green beans, carrots, or peas.

Serves: 4
Preparation time: 15 minutes
Cooking time: 25 minutes

2 tablespoons ghee
1 medium onion, sliced
4 whole cloves
3 green cardamom pods
1 small stick of cinnamon
2 bay leaves
1 teaspoon raisins
1^1/$_2$ cups basmati rice, washed and drained
Salt, to taste

1 Heat half the ghee in a small saucepan and fry the onion until well browned, for about 10 minutes. Stir frequently to prevent them from burning. Set them aside on kitchen towel.

2 Heat the remaining ghee in a separate pan and fry the spices and bay leaves for 1 minute. Add the raisins and the rice and stir for a couple of minutes. Season with salt and pour in 3 cups of hot water.

3 Bring to a boil, stir, reduce the heat, and cover. Simmer for 10 minutes and then turn off the heat and keep covered for another 10 minutes for the rice to fluff up in the steam. Serve hot, garnished with the fried onions.

fried puffy bread
luchis

These are exactly like the poories of northern and western India and are very popular all over Bengal. In fact a breakfast of luchi and subjee or vegetables is considered special. Luchis are also served as a part of a festive meal. One such time is Durga Puja, the important festival in honor of the Mother Goddess that is especially celebrated in Bengal.

Serves: 4
Preparation time: 15 minutes
Cooking time: 25 minutes

2^1/$_3$ cups all-purpose flour, plus extra for flouring
Sunflower oil for deep-frying
Salt, to taste

1 Put the flour in a shallow dish, make a well in the center and pour in 2 tablespoons of oil. Season with salt. Add enough water to make a stiff dough and knead well. Cover with a wet cloth and set aside for 30 minutes.

2 Make 8 equal-sized balls from the dough and roll each one out into a thin disc, flouring the board as necessary.

3 Heat the oil in a deep frying pan. When it is nearly smoking, fry 1 luchi at a time, turning it over until it is puffy and golden on both sides. Serve hot.

sweet and sour lentils
bengali dal

Enjoy this with luchis for a perfect Bengali meal. If you cannot get hold of mango powder, use 1 teaspoon of tamarind concentrate diluted in a few tablespoons of water. Channa dal takes a long time to cook. If you have the time to soak it overnight, do so as this will drastically reduce cooking times.

Serves: 4
Preparation time: 20 minutes + at least 1 hour soaking time
Cooking time: 1 hour

1²/₃ cups split gram lentils (channa dal)
1 teaspoon turmeric
Salt, to taste
2 teaspoons sugar
3 tablespoons sunflower oil
2 tablespoons panch phoron (page 160)
4 dried red chiles, seeded and crumbled
2 bay leaves
2 teaspoons mango powder (amchoor)
1 tablespoon raisins

1 Simmer the lentils in about 3 cups of hot water until soft and mushy. Add water as necessary to get a thick consistency, then stir in the turmeric, salt, and sugar. Blend well.

2 Heat the oil in a small pan and add the panch phoron. When it crackles, add the red chiles, bay leaves, mango powder, and raisins. Reduce the heat and pour the oil and the spices over the lentils.

3 Add water if needed to adjust the consistency which should be that of a thick soup. Bring to a boil once and serve hot.

spiced red lentils
mushur dal

Red lentils are available as whole or split. The whole ones are brown like puy lentils while the split ones are orangey-red. These cook very easily and do not need to be soaked. The consistency of the dal should be quite thick and soupy.

Serves: 4
Preparation time: 10 minutes
Cooking time: 30 minutes

³/₄ cup red lentils (masoor dal), washed and drained
Salt, to taste
¹/₂ teaspoon turmeric
2 fresh green chiles, finely chopped
2 tablespoons sunflower oil
2 dried red chiles
1 teaspoon panch phoron (page 160)
1 medium onion, chopped

1 Put the red lentils along with the salt, turmeric, and green chiles into a heavy saucepan with about 3 cups of hot water and bring to a boil. Reduce the heat and cook for about 15 minutes until the lentils are mushy. Remove from the heat and set aside.

2 Heat the oil in a large saucepan and add the red chiles and the panch phoran. As it turns dark, add the onion and fry until soft.

3 Add the cooked lentils and bring to a boil. Remove from the heat and serve hot with plain rice.

cauliflower fritters
phoolkopir bhaja

Vegetable fritters are found not just all over India but around the world. The onion pakora has become a popular snack everywhere. Spices make the fritters easy to digest.`

Serves: 4
Preparation time: 20 minutes
Cooking time: 25 minutes

For the batter:
1 cup chickpea flour
1/2 teaspoon chili powder
1 teaspoon turmeric
1 teaspoon cumin seeds
1/2 teaspoon ajowan seeds
Salt, to taste

Sunflower oil for deep-frying

11 ounces cauliflower, cut into medium-sized
  florets (about 4 cups)

1 Make a thick batter of all the batter ingredients and add water as needed to achieve the consistency of thick custard.

2 Heat the oil in a deep kadhai or frying pan until it is nearly smoking.

3 Dip each cauliflower floret in the batter and gently add to the hot oil. Reduce the heat to let the cauliflower cook through. Do this in batches, a few at a time, frying until golden, then drain on absorbent paper.

4 Serve hot with Pineapple Chutney (right) or tomato ketchup.

pineapple chutney
ananas chutney

Each year my grandmother would prepare a seasonal pineapple chutney that would make the house smell like a tropical paradise. I loved to eat this sweet confection with rotis at teatime when I got home from school. This is the Bengali version, rich with dried fruit and spices. It can be stored in the fridge, in an airtight container or jar, for up to 10 days.

Serves: 4
Preparation time: 25 minutes if using
  fresh pineapple
Cooking time: 15 minutes

1 tablespoon sunflower oil
1/2 teaspoon panch phoron (page 160)
2 dried red chiles
1 teaspoon raisins
2 dates, pitted and chopped
1 teaspoon peeled and freshly grated ginger
6 ounces fresh or canned pineapple (about
  1 cup), chopped (drained if using canned)
1 tablespoon lemon juice
Salt, to taste
Sugar, to taste

1 Heat the oil in a heavy-bottomed saucepan and add the panch phoron. When it crackles, add the chiles, then the raisins, dates, and ginger, and stir a couple of times.

2 Add the pineapple, and 5–6 tablespoons of water if using fresh pineapple, or juice if using canned pineapple. Cook over low heat for 5 minutes until the pineapple is quite mushy. Sprinkle in the lemon juice, season with salt and add sugar. Cook for another 2 minutes and remove from the heat. Cool and serve with any main meal.

cottage cheese in spiced sweet milk
rasmalai

Rasmalai is one of the most famous Indian desserts known outside of India. The one you eat in restaurants is usually commercially mass-produced and this homemade version is more crumbly and delicate. I hang up the paneer for quite a long time to make sure that it does not crumble up too much during the cooking. Sometimes I serve the rasmalai in mango-flavored milk—just add a little mango purée to the milk before serving.

Serves: 4
Preparation time: 10 minutes + 1 hour draining time
Cooking time: 45 minutes

2 quarts (8 cups) milk
Few drops of lemon juice
$^3/_4$ cup sugar
$^1/_2$ teaspoon ground cardamom seeds
Pinch of saffron
2 teaspoons sliced almonds and pistachios

1 Put 5 cups of the milk into a pan and bring it to a boil. Add the lemon juice and let the milk curdle. Hang up the curdled milk in some clean piece of cheesecloth and let the whey drain off for about 30 minutes.

2 In the meantime set 6 cups of water to boil in a large, shallow pan and add a few tablespoons of the sugar to it.

3 Take the paneer out of the cheesecloth and knead it lightly for about 1 minute. Shape it into balls the size of a small lime and flatten them slightly. You should get about 8 balls.

4 Reduce the heat under the boiling water and slip the balls in gently.

5 After about 10 minutes, drain and remove them. The water will go milky and bits will break away from the paneer balls but this is normal. Keep the drained paneer balls flat on a plate. They should be quite spongy.

6 In a separate pan, heat the rest of the milk and sugar. Cook it until it's reduced and quite thick, for about 30 minutes, taking care not to let it burn or boil over. This is done over a fairly low heat. Add the ground cardamom and the saffron.

7 Remove from the heat, let it cool, and gently add the paneer balls to the milk. Chill well and serve sprinkled with the sliced nuts.

yogurt balls in saffron syrup
ledikini

Bengali sweets are usually made with sugar syrup and therefore taste quite rich and sweet. Many Bengalis will take a leisurely stroll after dinner to the nearest sweet shop to select a dessert! There is a huge variety of desserts to tempt the eye and the palate.

Serves: 4
Preparation time: 10 minutes + 12 hours draining time
Cooking time: 45 minutes + 30 minutes steeping time

3 cups whole-milk yogurt
²/₃ cup fine semolina
¹/₂ teaspoon ground cardamom
1¹/₂ cups sugar
Pinch of saffron
Sunflower oil for deep-frying

1 Hang up the yogurt in a few thicknesses of clean cheesecloth for at least 12 hours, until it is quite dry and flaky.

2 Scoop out the hung yogurt into a mixing bowl and beat it to loosen it. Knead in the semolina and cardamom. Mix well to form a dough and set aside.

3 Now make the sugar syrup. Combine the sugar with 2¹/₄ cups of water in a heavy saucepan. Add the saffron. Bring to a boil and reduce the heat to a simmer until a single thread syrup forms. To check this, put a drop of the syrup onto a cold plate. Cool slightly and dab with your finger. When you lift your finger, a single thread of syrup should be seen. Remove from the heat and set aside.

4 Shape the dough into equal-sized balls the size of a large cherry. Heat the oil in a deep frying pan or kadhai. When it is nearly smoking hot, gently slip a few balls at a time into the hot oil. Fry them over low heat to prevent them from splitting and to cook them evenly, and turn them from time to time.

5 When they are brown, lift out, drain, and place on absorbent paper. When all the balls are fried, add them to the cool sugar syrup and let them steep for 30 minutes, then lift out and serve.

baby milk dumplings in rose syrup
rossogulla

In 1866, Nobin Chandra Das set up a small sweet shop in Calcutta and, being from a sugar trading family, conjured up a new sweet dipped in sugar syrup. This was the rossogulla. The story goes that a wealthy businessman's carriage stopped for some water at Das's shop. Das offered a rossogulla with the water and the businessman loved it, creating fabulous opportunities for the young store-owner. Rossogullas keep very well in the fridge so you could make them in advance if cooking for a party.

Serves: 4
Preparation time: 1 day
Cooking time: 30 minutes

2^1/$_2$ cups whole milk
Juice of 2 lemons
1 tablespoon all-purpose flour
^{3}/$_4$ cup sugar
2 tablespoons rose water

1 Bring the milk to boiling point in a heavy saucepan and add the lemon juice to the pan. The milk will begin to split. Reduce the heat and keep simmering until all the milk solids have separated. Line a large bowl with a few thicknesses of cheesecloth and pour the split milk into it. Lift the cloth out and drain off the whey. Hang it up over the sink to continue the draining. (I tie the cheesecloth bag to my kitchen faucet!)

2 When the milk solids are almost dry, put the bundle into a colander, press down with a weight, and let it drain for another 3–4 hours.

3 Once the solid cheese (paneer) has been formed, knead it with the flour to form a soft dough. Make small balls the size of large cherries from this dough. Set aside.

4 Now make the rose syrup. Boil the sugar and 1^1/$_2$ cups of water in a heavy saucepan. Reduce the heat and simmer until the syrup thickens and you get a single thread consistency. (Check by putting a drop on a cool plate and dabbing it carefully with your finger. If a thin thread of syrup rises with your finger, it is ready.)

5 Add the cheese balls and the rose water to the syrup. Cook over low heat for 10 minutes. Cool and serve.

frosted pastries
malpua

These sweet, crisp discs should be soft at the center and crispy at the edges. I like to serve them with a spoonful of cream and some fresh fruit. They are quite easy to make and keep quite well. Street stalls in some cities sell them freshly made, hot and fragrant. I think they taste good when cold as well.

Serves: 4
Preparation time: 20 minutes + 2 hours resting time
Cooking time: 30 minutes

2^3/$_4$ cups self-rising flour
3 tablespoons semolina
^{3}/$_4$ cup plain yogurt
Pinch of baking soda
Ghee or sunflower oil for frying
Few crushed pistachios

For the syrup:
^{3}/$_4$ cup sugar
^{3}/$_4$ cup water
1 teaspoon fennel seeds
1 teaspoon ground cardamom

1 Mix the flour, semolina, yogurt, and baking soda, adding a little water to make a thick batter. Then cover and leave in a warm place for about 2 hours.

2 In the meantime, make the syrup by mixing the sugar, water, and fennel seeds. Cook over high heat until a light syrup forms. Remove from the heat, add the ground cardamom, and set aside.

3 Heat the ghee or oil in a kadhai or deep frying pan. When it begins to smoke, lower the heat and pour in a ladleful of the batter. It will spread so shape it into a thick disc.

Fry, turning over once, until golden. Drain and arrange on a platter. Continue with the rest of the batter.

4 When all the discs are fried, pour the warm fennel syrup over them. Serve sprinkled with the pistachios.

sweet coconut crêpes
patishapta

My mother used to make these for Sunday breakfast and they always remind me of indulgent days when all one needs to think of is relaxation. The cardamom and nutmeg give these crêpes a real lift and you can add your favorite nuts for a bit of texture. The crêpe should be white and fine and, if you find it breaking up, add a couple of teaspoons of all-purpose flour to bind the batter.

Serves: 4
Preparation time: 30 minutes
Cooking time: 30 minutes

2¹/₃ cups rice flour
Salt, to taste
³/₄ cup jaggery or soft brown sugar
8 ounces freshly grated or dried, shredded
  coconut (about 1¹/₃ cups)
¹/₃ cup milk
¹/₂ teaspoon ground cardamom
¹/₂ teaspoon ground nutmeg
¹/₄ cup ghee or sunflower oil

1 Make a crêpe batter with the flour, salt, and as much water as necessary to create a pouring consistency. Set aside.

2 To make the filling, heat a heavy pan and melt the sugar or jaggery. Add the coconut and cook until the mixture is fully combined.

3 Pour in the milk and continue cooking until the mixture is thick. Then remove from the heat and stir in the spices.

4 To cook the crêpes, heat a few drops of the ghee or oil in a shallow frying pan. Reduce the heat and pour a ladleful of batter in the center, spreading it with the back of the ladle to make a thin disc. Cover and cook for 1 minute over low heat.

5 When the edges start to curl up, flip the crêpe and cook on the other side for 1 minute. Arrange some of the coconut mixture along the center of the crêpe and roll it up into a cylindrical shape. Serve warm.

panch phoron

Bengal lies in the northeast of India. Art, literature, food, and festivals are all an inseparable part of every Bengali person's life. The people are known for their passion for rice, and sweets made of clotted or burnt milk, flavored with rose water or saffron and soaked in sugar syrup or cold, sweet milk. The most popular blend of spices here is panch phoron—Bengal's equivalent of the Chinese five-spice powder. This mixture too has five different spices which are used either in their whole form or ground to a powder and this is used for flavoring lentils, legumes, or vegetables. Its unique aroma is bittersweet and powerful. Panch phoron is added to hot oil first before adding vegetables, lentils, or legumes. As it begins to splutter, the rest of the ingredients are dropped into the pan. Alternatively, it is fried in oil or ghee which is poured on top of a dish to flavor it. As with other blends, you can vary the ingredients according to taste.

My recipe for panch phoron is to mix equal quantities of:

Cumin seeds
Fennel seeds
Fenugreek seeds
Black mustard seeds
Nigella seeds

orange/red lentils
masoor dal

Orange lentils are the seeds of a bushy plant that grows in cold climates. When mature, the long pods in which the lentils are contained are plucked, dried, and threshed.

When left whole, the lentils are dark brown to greenish-black in color, round and flattish. The fairly thick skin conceals a pinkish-orange center. Split lentils are the familiar orange ones found in shops. These lentils are delicate in flavor and have a nutty, fresh taste. The whole lentils are chewy, muskier, and coarser.

Whole red lentils and split lentils have quite different qualities so when buying make sure you buy what is asked for in the recipe. Split red lentils are useful as they are fast cooking and make a quick, nutritious meal. Both the varieties store well for up to 6 months in a dry, airtight container.

yellow lentils
toor dal

The yellow lentils plant is a deep-rooted shrubby perennial which is grown from seed. The pods are dried in the sun or mechanically, and husked to separate the seeds, which are the lentils. In some parts of India, yellow lentils are slightly oiled to increase shelf-life, more so when the lentils are exported, and therefore Indian stores outside India usually stock the oily variety of yellow lentils.

These lentils are yellow and sold split into 2 round halves. The oily variety is sticky and glossy, the unoily one is matte. Yellow lentils are very easy to digest and have a pleasant, subtle, nutty flavor.

If you buy oily yellow lentils, soak them in hot water for a while and throw away the resulting cloudy, white liquid. Then wash the lentils several times to get rid of most of the oil. Yellow lentils store well for up to 6 months in clean, dry containers.

gram lentils (chickpeas)
channa dal

Gram, or Bengal gram as it is also known, is the most widely grown lentil in India. In the U.S. it is known as dried chickpeas or garbanzo beans. The bushy shrub bears seed-filled pods, each containing 2 or 3 lentils. They are picked in early winter when they turn ripe and brown. Then they are husked and left whole, split or ground into a flour called besan. This flour is used to make batter (as in fritters), as a thickening in curries, or is cooked with sugar to make many different sweets.

Matte and yellow, gram lentils resemble yellow lentils but are slightly bigger and coarser. They are stronger in taste than most other lentils with a nutty sweet aroma and flavor.

Good gram lentils should be plump and bright. Store in an airtight container for about 4 months.

mung beans
moong

Mung beans, or green gram, are the most versatile of all the lentils. The bean sprouts served in Chinese food are actually sprouted mung beans.

The small mung bean plant grows all over India as a rain-fed crop. The beans, which grow inside pods, are threshed out after the pods are dried—either on the plant or in the sun. Mung beans are left in their skin or split. There is also a variety which is split but left in the skin.

Whole mung beans, or green gram, are small, oval, and olive-green in color. When split, they are small, flattish, and yellow. Whole mung beans have a stronger flavor than the split ones. They are rather chewy and musky. The yellow, split mung beans are extremely easy to cook, need no soaking, and are easy to digest.

The whole beans and the split ones are quite different and are seldom interchangeable so you will need to get both, depending upon what you plan to make. Store in an airtight container for up to 4 months.

jaggery
gur

Sugar cane grows in abundance in the tropical heat of central India. During the manufacture of sugar from sugar cane, as the cane turns to crystal, several bi-products are formed: molasses, alcohol, and jaggery. Jaggery is dehydrated sugar cane juice and is produced mostly by small cultivators in huge crushers run by bullocks. The jaggery is not purified and therefore has all the quality of the juice itself. Jaggery is as important as sugar in Indian cooking. It has a special flavor that cannot really be substituted by sugar, although brown or Demerara sugar is the closest equivalent.

Jaggery ranges from mustard yellow to deep amber in color, depending upon the quality of the sugar cane juice. It is sticky but crumbles easily. Jaggery has a heavy, caramel-like aroma which is slightly alcoholic, like sweet sherry or port. The taste is very sweet and musky. It goes well with lentils and tamarind. You will find that jaggery is available in various sizes and wrapped in plastic or in jute cloth. Use within 6 months.

asafetida
hing

Although not native to India, asafetida has been an essential part of Indian cooking and medicine for ages. Due to its offensive smell it is also sometimes referred to as "devil's dung."

Asafetida is the dried latex from the rhizomes of several species of ferula or giant fennel. It is grown chiefly in Iran and Afghanistan from where it is exported to the rest of the world. In India it is cultivated in Kashmir. Asafetida is the product of a tall, smelly, perennial herb, with strong, carrot-shaped roots. In March or April, just before flowering, the stalks are cut close to the root. A milky liquid oozes out, which dries to form asafetida. This is collected and a fresh cut is made. This procedure continues for about 3 months, by which time the plant has yielded up to (2¼ pounds) of resin and the root has dried up.

Fresh asafetida is whitish and solid and gradually turns pink to reddish-brown on exposure to oxygen. It is ocher when sold commercially and the most widely used form is the fine yellow powder or granules. Asafetida has a pungent, unpleasant smell quite like that of pickled eggs, due to the presence of sulphur compounds. On its own it tastes awful but its powerful aroma complements lentils, vegetables, and pickles, completing the flavor of the dish. It is always used in small quantities—a tiny pinch added to hot oil before the other ingredients is enough to flavor a dish for 4.

Most commonly available boxed as powder or as granules, asafetida is also sold as a hard lump that needs to be crushed. It keeps well for up to a year.

fenugreek
methi

Ancient herbalists believed that fenugreek aided digestion. Even today the seeds are eaten to relieve flatulence, chronic cough, and diarrhea. Fenugreek the spice consists of small, hard, ocher, oblong seeds. The leaves of the plant are also eaten as a popular vegetable all over India. The whole plant has a pronounced, aromatic odor and the seeds smell of curry. Fenugreek is one of the most powerful Indian spices known for its aroma and lingering taste. It is an essential ingredient of curry powder.

The seeds are available whole, crushed, or powdered. The fresh stalks with leaves are sold in every Indian food store and the dried leaves, called kasuri methi are sold in packs, either whole or powdered. It is well worth buying kasuri methi—it is used as a flavoring and adds a very wholesome touch to meats, vegetables, and onion-based curries. Store the seeds as well as kasuri methi in dry jars. Use the seeds in 6 months, the dried leaves in 4.

nigella
(black onion seeds)
kalonji

The nigella plant is a relative of the delicate "love-in-a-mist" which decorates many gardens worldwide. In India, nigella is also known as black onion seed although the seeds have nothing to do with onions.

Nigella is the dried seed-like fruit of a small herb with wispy sage-colored leaves and graceful flowers which ripen into seed capsules. These are collected when ripe. They are then dried, crushed whole, and sifted to separate the seeds.

Nigella seeds are jet black with a matte finish like tiny chips of coal. They have a faint nutty, but bitter taste due to the presence of nigellin. Nigella goes beautifully with fish, in nan bread, and in salads. In west Bengal the most prolific spice blend is panch phoron, a mixture of five spices including nigella.

indian cottage cheese
paneer

Paneer is Indian cottage cheese and is neutral in taste. Unlike cottage cheese eaten in the west, commercially made paneer is firm, dry, and can be cleanly cut. It tastes delicious both fried or au naturel.

In India, the people of Punjab make the most wonderful paneer. The milk is first heated and then lemon juice is added to split it. The result is clotted milk and this is hung in muslin until all the liquid or whey has drained away, usually overnight. This homemade paneer is softer, wetter, and more like the cottage cheese we see in the West. This is because factory-made paneer is pressed down with heavier weights and so more of the liquid is squeezed out.

grains

The Indian kitchen uses a variety of grains. Rice is as common as wheat and is eaten whole or is milled into flour used for making batter and doughs, especially for festive sweets. Wheat flour is used daily. In most places in India, people still buy whole wheat, clean it, and take it to the nearest chakki or mill to make sure they get the freshest, purest flour possible. This whole wheat flour or "atta" is brownish and coarser than refined flour because it contains more bran and is used for making a number of rotis, parathas, and poories. The finer the whole wheat flour, the softer the rotis will be. Refined wheat flour, which is used for making certain breads, is fine, white, and soft.

Semolina is made by processing wheat into tiny grains. The wheat is cleaned, the wheatgerm is separated, and the remainder is coarsely milled into semolina. You can buy fine or coarse semolina. Fine semolina is used for recipes that require a smoother finish such as a south Indian snack called upma, a kind of savory cake sprinkled with fresh coconut and fragrant coriander. Coarse semolina is often made into a dessert with sugar, raisins, and ghee called halwa. Fish or vegetable patties are rolled in semolina before frying to give a crisp coating. Babies are fed a porridge made with semolina as a first weaning food.

In India corn is commonly called maize and is grown as a vegetable or for grinding into flour.

Coarse milling produces cornmeal and cornstarch, which are rich in carbohydrates. Cornstarch is fine, white, and soft whereas cornmeal is coarse, grainy, and pale yellow. When fried, both the flours become very crisp. Cornmeal is added to batters and vegetable stir-fries. Corn rotis or bread called "makke ki roti" are popular in Punjab and are traditionally served hot with spiced mustard greens during the cold winter months.

Other grains that are used include bajra and jowar, which are milled into a flour for thick rotis. Bajra and jowar flours are often combined to make bhakri or other breads. They are pounded together with spices, rolled out into thin discs, and dried to make poppadoms.

gourds

The gourd family has about 800 species and many of these are grown in India and some are available in the West. Historians claim that cultivation of these tropical plants began in Africa or India several thousand years ago. Gourds vary in size, shape, and color, but almost all have a distinctive skin and a multitude of seeds embedded in the inner flesh. Many gourds are hollowed out and dried to store water and food or used as musical instruments.

Some Indian gourds include "turai" or ridged gourd. The fruit has raised ridges along its length. As the fruits mature these, as well as the seeds within, harden and make the fruit dry and lifeless. The young fruits are cooked in stir-fries much like a zucchini. When preparing, peel the ridges thinly, but the remaining skin can be eaten. In some places in India, these discarded ridges are soaked in water and ground up into a delicious chutney with coconut and spices.

Karela or bitter melons are popular in spite of their intense bitter flavor and are often combined with onions and tomatoes. Their skin is bright green and knobbly when fresh and, as they mature, the skin turns yellow and the seeds start to turn orange. The flesh is white and cottony but can dry out in over-ripe fruits. There is a Chinese variety of bitter melon which is lighter in color and fatter, and a Thai variety, which is white. To prepare karela, slice thinly and soak in salted water for a couple of hours. Some people drink this bitter water as a tonic. It is a good vegetable to hollow out and fill with spiced mashed potatoes and can also be used in curries.

Dudhi or doodhi is also called bottle gourd. There are many varieties of different shapes and sizes and these grow on climbers in many domestic gardens. They have a smooth pale green skin and the inner flesh is white, spongy, and a bit like cucumber in taste. It is quite a bland watery vegetable and cannot be eaten raw. Dudhi is very versatile and can be made into curries, pancakes, or sweets such as halwa.

Petha or fuzzy melon looks like an uneven-skinned version of bottle gourd. It has a nipped center. It is made into a sweet called "petha" which is very sweet and translucent. Agra is most famous for this sweet.

Snake gourds are long and thin and can measure over 12 yards in length! They are plucked when very tender and flexible and weights are often placed on them while growing to keep them straight. If left to grow naturally, they end up curling around themselves like huge green snakes. This strange looking vegetable is chopped up and sold in manageable lengths. It cooks easily and is combined with lentils for texture and nutritional value.

Tindora, tendli, or ivy gourds are long oval fruits measuring only about 2 inches in length. They taste crunchy and cucumber-like and are quite fresh and juicy. Over-ripe tindora are red on the inside and can be bitter, in which case they need to be discarded. They are sliced lengthwise or in small discs and are used in stir-fries or pickles. They go very well with cashews, coconut, and garlic.

Tinda are smooth-skinned lemon-sized round gourds that are cooked with garlic and tomatoes and are quite popular in north Indian cooking.

Parwal or pointed gourds have a dark green striped skin and large seeds. The skin is quite coarse but edible. They taste wonderful when dusted with rice or wheat flour and deep-fried.

garlic and onions

There are 325 varieties of onion, all belonging to the lily family. Indian onions are white, pink, or purple and range from small to about the size of a tennis ball. There are also the small pearl onions that are used in south Indian "sambhar" or lentils. In Gujarat and Maharashtra they are combined with stuffed eggplants to add a hint of sweetness. Scallions are white with green leaves and have to be eaten fresh. They are cooked with gram flour to make a traditional Maharashtrian dish called zunka. The onions called for in most Indian recipes can be substituted with Spanish onions in the west. These are mild and juicy and add bulk as well as moisture to curries.

Onion is perhaps the most widely eaten vegetable in India and is grown on farms and in kitchen gardens. It contains an essential oil and organic sulphides which gives it a peculiar, sulphurous smell. This smell is released when the tissues of the onion are cut. The taste of raw onions is quite pungent with a hint of sweetness. When cooked, onions have a wholesome aroma and sweetish taste.

It is best to store onions in a cool, dry, airy place as any moisture will cause them to rot. In India, white onions are woven onto ropes quite like the way garlic can be sold in the West. Some onions seem to keep for weeks, while others become moldy and soft rather quickly. The reason lies in the moisture content. A firm dry onion will keep quite a bit longer than one that is soft and springy. Many people assume that it is good practice to store onions and potatoes together but this is not so. Potatoes have a lot of moisture and can give off a gas that causes onions to spoil more rapidly.

Peeling or chopping onions is never easy. In my many cooking classes and demos, this is the task that draws all the moans from participants because Indian cooking seems to need so many onions! When I was studying at the Catering College in Mumbai, we all had to work for a part of the week in the Quantity Kitchen producing about 500 meals a day. You can imagine the tears generated by bags and bags of onions! I have found that the best way to lessen the crying is to put onions into the fridge for a little while before chopping them. This seems to make the sulphur oils a bit more stable.

Onions are available all year round. They have diuretic properties and are often used to relieve catarrh in the bronchial tubes. A teaspoon of onion juice mixed with honey is even given to babies for this purpose.

Onions are used in every kind of Indian cooking to flavor, thicken, color, garnish, or accompany dishes. They can be boiled or fried and ground to a paste as a base for curries, fried until dark brown as a garnish or simply sliced, drizzled with lemon juice, and served as a side salad. They go well with tomatoes, ginger, garlic, meat, and potatoes.

Hailed as the "bulb of life," garlic was known to ancient physicians as an incomparable medicine. Garlic is a bulbous perennial herb of the onion family consisting of 6–30 individual bulbs called cloves. Several varieties of Indian garlic such as Poona, Nasik, and Madurai are popular all over the world. What one sees in the West is an Oriental variety called elephant garlic which is larger and milder than the small variety sold in India. Fresh garlic or garlic greens are grown in many household kitchens. They are wonderfully aromatic, more herb-like in aroma than bulbs of garlic, and in the winter they are combined with a mixture of vegetables to make a Gujarati delicacy called Undhiyoon. Garlic powder or flakes are also sold but do not have the power and potency of fresh garlic.

Garlic has an unmistakable and pungent aroma. It has a flavor that is much stronger than that of onion. The smell has an undernote of sulphur which is either loved or hated, as some people find its lingering smell distasteful. The taste can be quite sharp and biting and can increase the heat of a dish so do take this into account when adding the other spices to the pan.

Garlic is one of the most widely used ingredients in the world. In India it is used in curries, marinades, chutneys, vegetable dishes, barbecued meats, relishes, and countless other preparations. Each clove of garlic is first peeled, and then the flesh can be chopped, grated, or made into paste. Garlic can be eaten raw or cooked; when frying make sure that the oil is not too hot or the garlic will burn and taste acrid. A few cloves of garlic, roughly bruised, fried in a little hot oil and poured into a curry can give it a real lift. Garlic and ginger complement each other and are often used together. Ginger-garlic paste (page 11) uses equal quantities of each and can be stored successfully in the freezer in an airtight box for a couple of months. If you find that your curry is too mild and insipid, a teaspoonful of ginger-garlic paste is sure to give it a bit of life.

chiles

Given that they are used in almost every savory recipe from any part of the country, it is surprising that until about 400 years ago, chiles were unknown in India. They were introduced by the Portuguese at the end of the 15th century. Commercially, chiles, which are fruits of the capsicum species, are classified on the basis of their color, shape, and pungency, and over a hundred varieties are grown and eaten all over the world. Chiles have a strong, smarting aroma and their taste ranges from mild to dynamite. The level of heat is dependent upon the amount of capsaicin present in the seeds, veins, and skin of the chiles, and is not diminished by cooking, storing, or freezing. This is why generally, the smaller the chili, the seeds and veins being more concentrated, the hotter it is.

Chiles bring heat as well as fragrance to a dish. Contrary to expectation, many of India's hottest places boast of a fiery cuisine because chiles actually cool down the system in hot weather. The capsaicin dilates blood vessels to increase circulation and encourage perspiration. However, if you ever bite into a chile unexpectedly, don't reach for a pitcher of water—capsaicin is insoluble in water (like oil). Dairy products have the power to neutralize capsaicin so try yogurt or milk to calm the fire.

India is the largest producer of chiles today, contributing 25 percent of the total world production. They are available fresh, dried, powdered, flaked, in oil, in sauce, bottled, and pickled. When buying fresh chiles, look for crisp, unwrinkled, and glossy ones. Red chiles are often dried for the purpose of better storage although varieties such as the ivory white, hot

Kanthari chile are also used. The pungency can vary from the mild Kashmir chile and some dried south Indian varieties such as Tomato chiles and Byadagi chiles that give more color than heat, to the fiery birds eye chiles from the northeast and the dried Guntur chiles which have a dark red, thick skin and incredible firepower. As with all ground spices, chili powder loses its strength and sparkle after a few months. Whole dried chiles will keep for up to a year if stored in a dry, dark place. When they are to be used in curry pastes, they are first soaked in some warm water to soften them. I like to shake out the seeds before grinding them up as the seeds are hard and often stay whole.

Chiles are very high in vitamins A and C and have more vitamin C per gram than many

oranges. However, an inordinate intake of chiles can burn the lining of the stomach, so beware of overindulgence. I have seen many people in England eat more chiles than most Indians I know!

All chiles need to be treated with respect. The capsaicin in chiles is highly irritating to skin, so be careful when preparing them. Try to avoid contact with the inside of the fruit and wash your hands with soap and water immediately after use. To reduce the pungency of chiles, discard the seeds and soak the rest in cold salted water. For maximum fire, slice the chiles and leave the seeds in. To prepare dried chiles, remove the stems and shake out the seeds. They can also be torn into bits, soaked in warm water, and ground to a paste for curries and sauces.

rice

Although India grows hundreds of varieties of rice such as the mango-perfumed ambemohur or the short-grained kolum, the flavor of basmati rice is celebrated the world over. Its name conjures up visions of lush, green paddy fields watered by the snow-fed rivers of the Himalayas. Basmati is considered to be the king of rice and as such, in India, it is reserved for special occasions or particular dishes. India was one of the earliest countries to grow rice. From here it traveled first to Egypt, then via Greece, Portugal, and Italy, to America. Historians estimate that it was first cultivated at least 3,000 years ago. Rice has always been a symbol of plenty in Hindu tradition. According to custom, married women in India are honored and wished a life of plenty by presenting them with a coconut, a handful of rice, and a length of fabric on festive occasions. The throwing of rice is associated with all weddings, whether Hindu, Christian, or Islamic.

Rice is gluten-free, making it an ideal food for babies or those with wheat or gluten intollerances. It is also cholesterol free and low in sodium unless you add salt to the cooking water (I never do this). It is rich in protein and contains all eight amino acids but it is poor in the amino acid lysine, which is found in beans, making the combination highly nutritious.

The grains of basmati rice are white, long, and very silky to touch. They are even in size and clean looking. The fragrance is unmistakable. Rich and wholesome, it has a pure scent and a fresh, uncluttered taste. It is available whole or as broken grains which are much cheaper.

Broken basmati is used in dishes that require a sticky texture such as rice pudding or for recipes that require the grinding up of rice as in batters. Rice flour is also used for batters or to coat vegetables when deep-frying them. It is made with cheaper varieties of rice. Rice is like wine—it gets better with age. Good basmati is left to mature in controlled conditions for up to 10 years. Old rice cooks better and remains fluffy whereas new rice becomes sticky when cooked. The only way to know whether the rice is old is to ask, but most brands of packaged rice in the West are suitable. Store in the package that the rice comes in or transfer to an airtight container and store for up 3 months.

Although there are as many ways of cooking perfect rice as there are rice eaters, one way is to wash the rice thoroughly until the water runs clear. Put it with double the quantity of fresh water into a heavy saucepan, bring to a boil and stir well. Reduce the heat, cover, and simmer for 10 minutes. Turn off the heat and let it sit in its steam for another 5 minutes. There is a saying in India that perfectly cooked rice should be like two brothers, close but not stuck together. Indians always serve rice piping hot and most often with lentils, beans, or a curry. Dal and rice is a staple meal in most of India. Basmati rice is made into rich biryanis, pilafs, sweets, stuffings, and snacks.

It is important to store cooked rice properly. It must be refrigerated soon after it has cooled down as it is easily contaminated. Also, I like to cook only the amount needed for each meal because once refrigerated, the starch amylase present in cooked long grain rice tends to toughen up and make the rice hard.

turmeric

One of the most traditional and versatile of spices used in Indian cooking, turmeric is the very heart and soul of any curry. This key ingredient is used daily in every part of India as its unique color, due to the presence of the pigment curcumin, and flavor enriches every regional cuisine. Turmeric is used prolifically in a host of Indian dishes ranging from appetizers, lentils, meats, and vegetables. It has also been used for centuries as a curative and cleansing agent. Since early times, it has been associated with purification so that even today, an Indian bride and groom are ritually anointed with turmeric as part of a cleansing ceremony, after which they do not leave the house until the wedding.

Turmeric has an earthy, sensual fragrance reminiscent of the aridness of vast fields parched in a hot Indian summer. On its own, it has a musky, dry taste, but it is used wholeheartedly in Indian cooking for its wonderful quality of enhancing and balancing the flavors of all the other ingredients. However, be careful not to use turmeric when cooking green vegetables as they will turn dull and taste bitter.

Store turmeric in a dry jar and use within 4 months or it may lose its vibrancy. Be careful while storing and using turmeric; it will stain hands and clothes quite quickly. Only cured turmeric has the aroma and color (chiefly due to the presence of the pigment curcumin) necessary for cooking.

cumin

Cumin the spice has been known to man since Biblical times. Sometimes confused with caraway or nigella, cumin is an important spice in its own right and one that makes a happy addition to almost every Indian savory dish.

Cumin seeds are really the fruits of the herb. They are elongated, oval, and long. They range from sage green to tobacco brown in color and have longitudinal ridges. During the drying process, some fine stalks invariably get left on, so cumin appears slightly bristly. Another variety of cumin is black cumin or kala jeera, shahi jeera, or siya jeera. The seeds are dark brown to black and are smaller and finer than cumin. The smell of cumin is distinctive. It can be described as peculiar, strong, and bitter and is usually loved or hated. Cumin has a warm, somewhat bitter taste.

It is available whole as seeds or crushed to a powder which is often blended with ground coriander to form a widely used mixture called dhana-jeera. This combination is one of the essential spice blends used in Indian cooking.

Toasted cumin powder gives a lift to many curries and yogurt-based raitas. It is not at all difficult to make this at home. Roast the seeds in a frying pan until they change color and crush them into a fine toasty powder in a mortar. Roasting the cumin releases and enriches its earthy flavor. As with all other spices, store cumin in a dry place away from light. The ground cumin is best used within 3 months.

coriander (cilantro)

Most Indian cooks will not allow a curry to leave their kitchen without a good sprinkling of fresh, fragrant coriander leaves, also known as cilantro. This pretty herb is the most commonly used garnish in the northern and western parts of India, and adds a dewy green touch to red or brown curries. Seeds of the coriander plant are the spice. Coriander is perhaps one of the first spices known to man and has been around for over 3,000 years. It finds mention in ancient Sanskrit texts and in the Bible where the color of manna is likened to that of coriander seeds.

Coriander leaves and the seeds are completely different from one another with regard to aroma and flavor. The leaves taste and smell fresh and fruity with a hint of ginger. The seeds, on the other hand, have a sweet, heady aroma with a subtle whiff of pine and pepper.

Little bunches of fresh coriander (cilantro) are commonly available at supermarkets. It looks quite like parsley but the test lies in the aroma—parsley has a more delicate smell than cilantro.

Coriander seeds have many healing properties. An infusion of the seeds is cooling and helps reduce fever. Suited to almost every savory Indian dish, coriander (the spice and the herb) is used daily in curries, chutneys, soups, and drinks. The fresh green chutney made by grinding coriander leaves, coconut, ginger, garlic, and spices is a popular sandwich spread or meal accompaniment. It is also served in Indian restaurants all over the world.

captions to photographs

Page 1 Golkonda Fort, Hyderabad, Andra Pradesh.

2/3 Rann of Kutch, Rabari woman (nomad) carrying water to her village.

6 a woman carries leafy branches she uses for animal feed

7 Vegetables for sale in southern Indian market.

8 Dakshineswar Kali Temple, near Kolkata (Calcutta), built in 1847 on the banks of the River Hoogly.

9 roadside stalls in Dacres Lane, Calcutta. Famous for tasty but basic lunches visited by office workers.

10 a group of cooks prepare chapatis which will feed visitors for Baisakhi Day (Harvest Festival in Punjab)

11 Udaipur City Palace. The bedroom of the Maharana Bhopal Singh born 1884, crowned 1930, died 1958. He was disabled from polio, you can see his wheelchair and bed. He tried to live a simple life with simple possesions.

12 At a water well near the town of Alkalkot in Maharashtra

15 Dakshineswar Kali Temple, near Kolkata (Calcutta), built 1847, on the banks of the River Hoogly. The temple is dedicated to the goddess Bhavatarini (Kali). This Temple is where the famous 19th century Hindu saint Ramakrishna attained his spiritual vision of the unity of all religions.

16 Irrigating plants on a plantation near Panaji, Goa

17 Harvesting coconuts in Kerala. The men climb up using a rope around their ankles and the tree.

20 The central Pillar of the Diwan-i-Khas (assembly hall) in Fatehpur Sikri, Rajasthan. The Emperor Akbar (ruled 1556-1605) sat above the pillar and his ministers on the balconies, with spectators standing below.

21 Pounding of turmeric in a granite bowl. Bhatoli Village, in the Yamuna Valley.

28 Bhatoli Village, women cook rice and dal over the "chula" under the verandah of their house

33 Presenting jaggery "cakes" made from sugar cane.

36 Jaggery "gur" making from sugar cane. Cottage industry. Three large concrete vats are heated from underneath. Sugar cane juice is boiled to extract sugar and in the purification process, thickening liquid is scooped from vat to vat.

40 Harvesting rice by cutting it with a scythe and laying the cut grain in the field to dry.

49 Rann of Kutch, Rabari woman (nomad) carrying water and crossing an irrigation channel.

53 Worker in a vegetable market carrying sacks of potatoes.

56 Dried basmati rice stalks with the grain attached are collected and bundled into sheafs.

59 New Delhi, Lodi Gardens, a monument from the Lodi Dynasty (1451-1526).

62 Udaipur, Rajasthan, view from City Palace to the luxury Lake Palace Hotel in Lake Pichola.

68 The last corn of the season is being husked for the cooking of rotis.

77 Two farm workers cut the ripe basmati rice.

81 Rann of Kutch, Jambouri viallage. A herder returns.

92 Rann of Kutch. Nomadic Rabari children in traditional costumes at their campsite.

95 Creative display of fruits for juicing. Chowpatti Beach, Mumbai.

96 Pouring milk into urns. Village near Anand, Gujarat.

98/99 Men carrying water on their way to Pushkar, Rajasthan.

102 Qutb Shahi Tomb near Hyderabad, Andhra Pradesh.

103 Backwaters of Kerala near Alleppy. Converted rice (transport) boats, now luxury houseboats "kettuvalla", operated by long bamboo poles, take tourists through the canals to view backwater life.

107 Kerala Temple, the elephant festival, Maradu Village, north of Cochin. The goddess Badhrakalan is symbolized by the golden shield on the biggest and tallest elephant, to the tune of drums and trumpets. Brahmins rise peacock feather fans and sheep's tail whisks.

110 Harvesting coconuts in Kerala. The men climb up using a rope around their ankles and the tree.

112 Banana tree in Kerala

117 Vegetable plantation, Goa.

121 Friday market in Mapusa, Goa.

123 Figure along one of the four Ratha Temples in Mamallampuram (7th century), 28 miles south of Chennai.

126 In the courtyard of a private house near Pondicherry, Tamil Nadu. Cooking of Pongal rice, during the Pongal Harvest Festival.

130 Chinese fishing nets at the northern tip of Fort Cochin, Cochin, Kerala.

136 Backwaters near Allepy, Kerala. A boat load of dried palm fronds is paddled past an old Catholic Church.

138 Catholic Church "Our Lady of the Immaculate Conception," Panaji, Goa.

142 Preparations for a temple festival in Bhubaneshwar, Orissa.

143 Rice fields along the foothills of the Himalayas.

145 Morning flower market close to the entrance of the Howrah Bridge, Kolkata (Calcutta), West Bengal.

150 Woman pilgrim performing a water ritual at the seaside of Puri, Orissa.

153 Vegetable market in Kolkata (Calcutta).

157 Kolkata (Calcutta), Javardpore Municiple Market. Shopping for vegetables.

161 View of the Jagannath Temple in Puri, Orissa, which is inaccessible for non-Hindus.

166 Baisakhi harvest festival. Bhangra dancers perform in wheat fields, wearing tradional Punjabi folk dress. Baisakhi, on 13th April, also celebrates the beginning of the New Year in Punjab.

171 Rice and spice emporium, southern India

173 Vegetable plantation, Panaji, Goa

index